JAGUAR
C TYPE AND D TYPE

ISBN 1 84155 759 5
13 ISBN 978-1-84155-759-5

C P Press

www.cppress.co.uk

Contents

Jaguar C-Type Racing Record

Date	Race	Drivers	Position
8 Mar 53	Sebring 12 Hours (Car no. 74 completed 162 laps)	Sherwood Johnston/ Bob Wilder	3rd
8 Mar 53	Sebring 12 Hours (Car no. 311 completed 155 laps)	Bob Gegan/ Harry Gray	4th
13-14 Jun 53	Le Mans 24 Hours (Car no. 18 completed 304 laps)	Tony Rolt/ Duncan Hamilton	1st
13-14 Jun 53	Le Mans 24 Hours (Car no. 17 completed 300 laps)	Stirling Moss/ Peter Walker/Tony Rolt	2nd
13-14 Jun 53	Le Mans 24 Hours (Car no. 19 completed 297 laps)	Peter Whitehead/ Ian Stewart	4th
13-14 Jun 53	Le Mans 24 Hours (Car no. 20 completed 275 laps)	Roger Laurent/ Charles de Tornaco	9th
26-27 Jul 53	Spa-Francorchamps 24 Hours (Car no. 19 completed 242 laps)	James Scott-Douglas/ Guy Gale	2nd
26-27 Jul 53	Spa-Francorchamps 24 Hours (Car no. 18 completed 231 laps)	Herman Roosdorp/ Toni Ulmen	3rd
30 Aug 53	Nürburgring 1000kms (Car no. 53 completed 44 laps)	Ian Stewart/ Ray Slavdori	2nd
30 Aug 53	Nürburgring 1000kms (Car no. 54 completed 41 laps)	John Lawrence/ Jimmy Stewart	6th
30 Aug 53	Nürburgring 1000kms (Car no. 56 completed 35 laps)	Kasimir Olislaegers/ Charles de Keerle	20th
5 Sep 53	Tourist Trophy (GB) (Car no. 7 completed 107 laps)	Stirling Moss/ Peter Walker	4th
5 Sep 53	Tourist Trophy (GB) (Car no. 12 completed 102 laps)	Joe Kelly/ Jack Fairman	8th
24 Jan 54	Buenos Aires 1000kms (Car no. 22 completed 100 laps)	James Scott-Douglas/ Ninian Sanderson	4th
24 Jan 54	Buenos Aires 1000kms (Car no. 18 completed 79 laps)	Masten Gregory/ Dale Duncan	14th
12-13 Jun 54	Le Mans 24 Hours (Car no. 16 completed 277 laps)	Roger Laurent/ Jacques Swaters	4th
11 Sep 54	Tourist Trophy (Car no. 11 completed 82 laps)	Jacques Swaters/ Roger Laurent	16th
11 Sep 54	Tourist Trophy (Car no. 10 completed 76 laps)	Joe Flynn/ Torrie N. Large	25th
13 Mar 55	Sebring 12 Hours (Car no. 14 completed 162 laps)	Russ Boss/ Jake Kaplan	12th
13 Mar 55	Sebring 12 Hours (Car no. 12 completed 155 laps)	Loyal Katskee/ Roger Wing	17th

Jaguar D-Type Racing Record

Date	Race	Drivers	Position Time
12-13 Jun 54	Le Mans 24 Hours (Car no. 14 completed 301 laps)	Tony Rolt/ Duncan Hamilton	2nd
11 Sep 54	Tourist Trophy (GB) (Car no. 6 completed 87 laps)	Ken Wharton/ Peter Whitehead	5th
11 Sep 54	Tourist Trophy (GB) (Car no. 20 completed 79 laps)	Stirling Moss/ Peter Walker	18th
13 Mar 55	Sebring 12 Hours (Car no. 19 completed 182 laps)	Mike Hawthorn/ Phil Walters	1st
11-12 Jun 55	Le Mans 24 Hours (Car no. 6 completed 307 laps)	Mike Hawthorn/ Ivor Bueb	1st
11-12 Jun 55	Le Mans 24 Hours (Car no. 10 completed 296 laps)	Jacques Swaters/ Johnny Claes	3rd
17 Sep 55	Tourist Trophy (GB) (Car no. 1 completed 81 laps)	Mike Hawthorn/ Desmond Titterington	Not running at finish
24 Mar 56	Sebring 12 Hours (Car no. 14 completed 188 laps)	Bob Sweikert/ Jack Ensley	3rd
24 Mar 56	Sebring 12 Hours (Car no. 16 completed 176 laps)	Alfonso Gomez Mena/ Santiago Gonzalez	
24 Mar 56	Sebring 12 Hours (Car no. 11 completed 168 laps)	Briggs Cunningham/ John Gordon Bennett	12th
24 Mar 56	Sebring 12 Hours (Car no. 8 completed 162 laps)	Mike Hawthorn/ Desmond Titterington	Not running at finish
27 May 56	Nürburgring 1000kms (Car no. 7 completed 43 laps)	Mike Hawthorn/ Desmond Titterington	Not running at finish
28-29 Jul 56	Le Mans 24 Hours (Car no. 4 completed 300 laps)	Ron Flockhart/ Ninian Sanderson	1st
28-29 Jul 56	Le Mans 24 Hours (Car no. 5 completed 284 laps)	Jacques Swaters/ Freddy Rousselle	4th
28-29 Jul 56	Le Mans 24 Hours (Car no. 1 completed 280 laps)	Mike Hawthorn/ Ivor Bueb	6th
12 Aug 56	Swedish Grand Prix (Car no. 16 completed 145 laps)	Peter Whitehead/ Graham Whitehead	6th
20 Jan 57	Buenos Aires 1000kms (Car no. 14 completed 95 laps)	Roberto Mieres/ Ninian Sanderson/ Alberto Rodriguez-Larreta	4th

Jaguar D-Type Racing Record

Date	Race	Drivers	Position Time
23 Mar 57	Sebring 12 Hours (Car no. 5 completed 193 laps)	Mike Hawthorn/ Ivor Bueb	3rd
23 Mar 57	Sebring 12 Hours (Car no. 7 completed 188 laps)	Walt Hansgen/ Russ Boss	5th
26 May 57	Nürburgring 1000kms (Car no. 10 completed 43 laps)	Ron Flockhart/ Jack Fairman	8th
26 May 57	Nürburgring 1000kms (Car no. 9 completed 42 laps)	Ivor Bueb/ John Lawrence/ Keith Hill	11th
26 May 57	Nürburgring 1000kms (Car no. 11 completed 40 laps)	Ninian Sanderson/ Richard Steed/ John Lawrence	16th
22-23 Jun 57	Le Mans 24 Hours (Car no. 3 completed 327 laps)	Ivor Bueb/ Ron Flockhart	1st
22-23 Jun 57	Le Mans 24 Hours (Car no. 15 completed 319 laps)	John Lawrence/ Ninian Sanderson	2nd
22-23 Jun 57	Le Mans 24 Hours (Car no. 17 completed 317 laps)	Jean Lucas/ Jean-Marie Brousselet	3rd
22-23 Jun 57	Le Mans 24 Hours (Car no. 16 completed 310 laps)	Paul Frere/ Freddy Rousselle	4th
22-23 Jun 57	Le Mans 24 Hours (Car no. 4 completed 299 laps)	Masten Gregory/ Duncan Hamilton	6th
11 Aug 57	Swedish Grand Prix (Car no. 10 completed 132 laps)	Alain de Changy/ Claude Dubois	5th
11 Aug 57	Swedish Grand Prix (Car no. 1 completed 129 laps)	John Lawrence/ Archie Scott-Brown	8th
11 Aug 57	Swedish Grand Prix (Car no. 2 completed 126 laps)	Ninian Sanderson/ Jack Fairman	11th
1 Jun 58	Nürburgring 1000kms (Car no. 10 completed 41 laps)	Jack Fairman/ John Lawrence	9th
13 Sep 58	Tourist Trophy (GB) (Car no. 4 completed 143 laps)	Masten Gregory/ Innes Ireland	5th
13 Sep 58	Tourist Trophy (GB) (Car no. 6 completed 142 laps)	Duncan Hamilton/ Peter Blond	6th
13 Sep 58	Tourist Trophy (GB) (Car no. 12 completed 135 laps)	Jonathan Sieff/ Maurice Charles	9th
5 Sep 59	Tourist Trophy (GB) (Car no. 7 completed 209 laps)	Ron Flockhart/ John Bekaert	7th

That Exciting New Jaguar

FULL DETAILS OF THE 3½-LITRE XK120 TYPE C

ALREADY it will have been realized that the designation Type C denotes a fresh version of the famous XK120, intended purely for competition and racing purposes. It consists of standard XK components rearranged in a different short and rigid triangulated steel tube frame, with special suspension and steering suitable for actual racing. The normal XK120, as was explained when that car was first introduced, was never intended as a racing car. It was to be one of the fastest open two-seater production cars offered to the public, and to that end it was given comfortable suspension and a flexible ease of performance which would appeal just as much to the experienced driver who enjoys the thrills of handling a tremendous acceleration, as to the devotee of ultra high speed. The XK120 leaped straight into popularity. It has proved to be so good that it quickly found a way into all kinds of competition, and has scored an impressively long series of successes.

As a result of this, owners, particularly in America, began to take the XK120 into competition with specially prepared lightweight "hot rods," when naturally it was handicapped by the weight of its luxury as a fast road touring car. Requests began to come in from the U.S.A. for information on tuning the XK120 to higher speeds still, which, of course, can be done, as explained in the Jaguar Service Bulletin No. 95 (reference to which was made in The Autocar of June 22). But it was decided that, if enthusiasts really wanted to go in for all-out catch-as-catch-can sports car races and competitions, the best thing was to give them a lightened new version of the XK120 made for the job, and for that job only, which meant a chassis suitable for speeds of 150 m.p.h. or more, and for handling at ultra high speeds.

And so, about eight months ago, design for the Type C was put in hand.

It is a stark competition car. Its seating accommodation is limited, it is not provided with hood or screens, it has only one door, on the driving side, and the amenities normally desired for general touring purposes have been dispensed with, in order to assist in reducing weight. It is not a dual-purpose car like the standard XK120. It will be put into limited production only, and it is not likely to be available for the home market in the foreseeable future. But what it has done already is to win a classic race first time out, the 24 Hours at Le Mans, against the best that the world can produce. (Impressions of the winning car appeared in The Autocar last week.) The price of the XK120 Type C will not be known until overseas deliveries can be made.

In laying out the design of the chassis, the primary consideration was to improve the ratio of power-to-weight by reducing the weight of the whole car and increasing the power output of the engine, in order to gain in acceleration as well as higher speed. In order to express these gains to the best advantage in competition and racing, the cornering ability had to be stepped up, and that entailed a stiffer but not a heavy frame construction, quicker and more positive steering, and a more controlled suspension.

Coming now to details, the engine is the same, in general, as the well-known 3½-litre six-cylinder 83 × 106 mm (3,442 c.c.), as shown in the specification. It has, however, the tuning modifications which are described in the service bulletin, and which include an 8 to 1 or 9 to 1 compression ratio according to the fuel which will be used. Different pistons are fitted to suit the different ratios. Both inlet and exhaust camshafts have high-lift cams, the ignition timing is advanced, and a special distributor head is used. The needles used in the carburettor are special, and "hot" sparking plugs are fitted. A lighter flywheel is used, and also a special high-speed crankshaft damper. A dual exhaust system is an

The steering wheel has a telescopic column for adjustment. On the facia the two main instruments are speedometer and rev counter of large size. The rev counter reads up to 6,500 r.p.m., and the section between 5,700 and 6,500 is coloured red. On the left of these are the ignition switch and ammeter, and on the right the fuel gauge and oil and water gauges. The gear lever is central and is carried on a shorter tunnel than in the XK.

All the front panelling hinges up to give remarkable accessibility.

important feature. The clutch has a special assembly, with a solid centre and linings riveted and cemented to the plate, to deal with racing starts. Much of the work of increasing the power output of the engine was carried out in conjunction with Mr. Henry Weslake.

When a car is to be capable of exceedingly high speeds it is essential that the construction be as rigid as possible, otherwise it will be difficult to control with that precision which the driver needs on curves and corners, and may also be uncertain during maximum acceleration and maximum braking. With the intention of providing this rigidity and at the same time not being too heavy, the Type C frame is a structure quite different from the more orthodox XK, and is a very interesting design. When laying out a touring car the designer has to consider the comfort of the occupants, not only for riding, but also for the simple matter of getting easily in, and subsiding gracefully into an armchair seat. That means doors. But when designing a competition or racing car, so long as the driver can leap hurriedly in, and compose himself for action in the

briefest time, that is enough, and doors can be reduced to one, and that only a shallow affair.

This quite simple aspect has a very definite bearing on the design of the frame as a whole, because it allows room for a structure of increased vertical height just at a point where rigidity is much needed, but is apt to be lacking, on most open two-seater cars with two doors. With these points in mind the Type C frame can be studied. Perhaps the easiest way to grasp the meaning of the forest undergrowth of steel tubes which appear in the sketch of this frame is to consider first the central part, around which the scuttle is situated. It will be seen that there is a tubular centre section framework more or less in the shape of a rectangular box lying laterally across the structure. This centre section is triangulated in three directions, laterally, horizontally, and longitudinally. The legs of the driver will be inside this box, and the front of it will be closed off with a steel bulkhead to divide it from the engine compartment, and to add stiffness.

Projecting forward from the centre section there is on each a triangulated girder of steel tube, forming, as it were, a horizontal pyramid. The outer side of each pyramid is also diagonally braced in the vertical plane. The apexes of the two pyramids are joined by the front cross-member structure, consisting of upper and lower box section laterals, and a V-shaped centre piece. This structure is further braced by an aft cross tube at the top, and diagonal foot bracings. Top and bottom of the front cross-member structure are brackets which provide the anchorage for the lateral links of

the front independent suspension, and the lower bracket on each side contains the front end of the longitudinal torsion bar, the tail of which is adjustably located in a bracket on the lower cross tube of the main centre section of the frame. It will be seen that this construction provides for rigidity between the front cross-member component and the centre section in every direction,

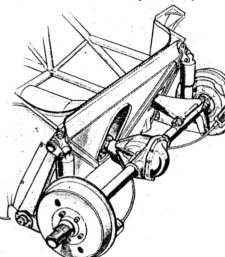

Rear suspension: The axle casing is located by underslung longitudinal links, the fulcrums of which are attached to a transverse torsion bar spring. The triangular torque-reaction member, on the right side above the axle end, prevents lateral movement, and, being at maximum distance from the axis of the propeller-shaft, imposes the maximum resistance to lift and spin of the right side wheel.

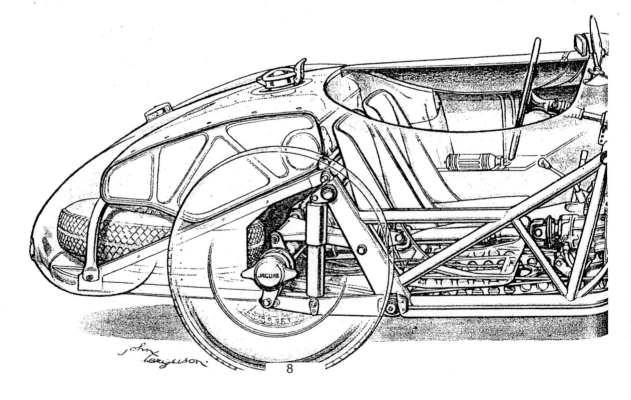

8

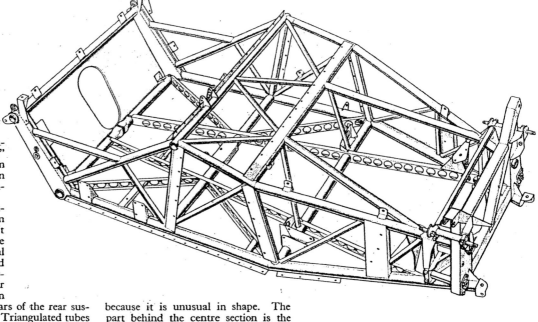

Frame of the Jaguar XK120C, which combines lightness with most carefully planned rigidity. The design of this structure is explained in the description.

lateral, vertical, longitudinal, "lozenge," and torsional. In the space between the pyramids the engine is mounted.

Now to look backwards from the main centre section: It will be seen that the lower longitudinal tubes of the forward part continues rearward to a tubular cross - member, in which the torsion bars of the rear suspension are housed. Triangulated tubes run down from the top of the centre section to meet this cross-member, and are further braced with diagonals. Running diagonally upwards and rearwards on each side are box section members, joined at the top by a cross tube, the space between them being filled by a steel bulkhead with a large slot in it for the tail of the propeller-shaft and the nose piece of the final drive case. It will be noticed that from the front cross-member to the centre of the back cross-member there are channel section runners, plentifully perforated for lightness. These, too, are diagonally braced, and carry the steel flooring. They also serve as "anti-lozenge" ties.

This frame needs a little explanation because it is unusual in shape. The part behind the centre section is the place where the driver has his bucket seat, with its back adjacent to the slotted bulkhead. The X-shaped members on each side occupy the space where the doors of an ordinary car would be situated, so at this point the frame retains its strength, and is fully triangulated right up to the point where the back axle is attached. There is reached another very interesting part of the design, the rear suspension.

The rear axle is a tubular type with an offset hypoid bevel final drive, and an open propeller-shaft with Hardy Spicer needle roller-bearing universal joints. Below each end of the axle casing is a downwardly depending bracket, at the foot of which is a link

A multiplicity of small tubes forms the main structure of the new type C Jaguar. Rack and pinion steering, mounted to the rear of the wheel centre lines, is operated from the steering column via a universal joint. Fresh cool air is conveyed to the twin S.U. carburettors by means of a large duct of rectangular section. Behind the rear damper can be seen the reaction member which enables the torque developed by the engine to assist in keeping both rear wheels on the ground, thereby considerably improving the getaway from rest.

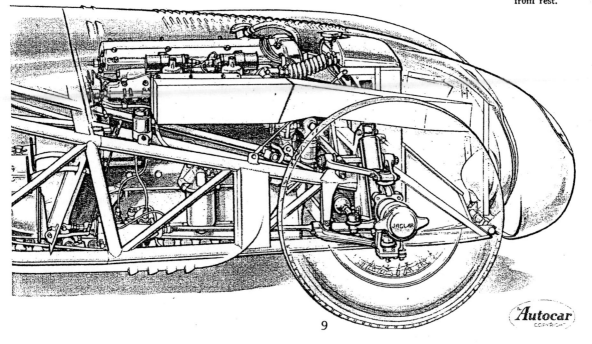

Autocar

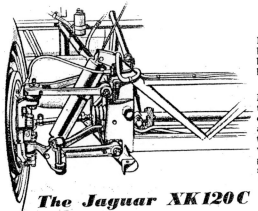

Left : Front suspension, with wide-based wishbones, longitudinal torsion bars and large Newton dampers, behind which the rack and pinion steering gear can be seen.

Right : Automatic adjustment of the Lockheed brakes. The shoes are coupled by a tie bar ; one end slides, and has a fine tooth ratchet passing through a housing. The ratchet is free when the shoes are expanding but engages on the nearest tooth when the shoes move into the " off " position.

The Jaguar XK120 C . . .

running forwards to a fulcrum anchorage at the back of the frame, these anchorages being attached to the ends of the rear cross tube of the frame as already described. The fulcrum of each link is splined to the outer end of a torsion bar spring, concealed in the cross-member and anchored in the centre of it. The foot of a telescopic hydraulic damper is attached towards the end of each link, and the head of the damper is hinged to the end of the upper lateral tube of the back of the frame structure. Hinged above the axle on the right-hand side, that is, just behind the driver, is a wide triangular link, with its fulcrum parallel to the axle, and its apex hinged to the back of the frame. This is the torque reaction member, and the purpose of mounting it to one side is to reduce the lift of the axle on one side when violent accelerations of the car are taking place; otherwise one rear wheel tends to lift and spin. The drivers in the race were enthusiastic about the effectiveness of this component.

The structure of the frame appears to end suddenly with the after bulkhead behind the driving compartment. Actually there is a subsidiary tail frame attached to this bulkhead, in a manner rather like the outrigger mounting of an engine in an aircraft. The tail frame carries the 40-gallon fuel tank, and a spare wheel beneath it, all concealed in a streamline tail fairing.

The whole outfit is relatively easily removable.

Similar in principle to that of the XK120, the independent front suspension consists of lateral wishbones and longitudinal torsion bar springs, controlled by large size 2in diameter Newton telescopic hydraulic dampers. The outer ends of the wishbones have spherical sockets which embrace ball heads at the top and bottom of the stub axle "fork," so that this fork becomes the steering swivel as well as forming the strut between the ends of the wishbones. The details of the Type C suspension are shown in one of the sketches, and it may be noted that the lower wishbones are somewhat shorter than on the XK, with a wider base. The two independent systems are cross coupled by a torsion anti-sway bar. Another material difference is that a rack and pinion steering gear is used. The purpose is to provide a light and direct steering which is quick in action. The steering wheel has a telescopic adjustment, and the column has a universal joint at the foot.

Built into the bonnet top are two ducts, with orifices which flank the radiator. One of these ducts conveys fresh frontal air under wind pressure to the filter box of the twin S.U. carburettors; the other plays cool air on the dynamo.

It will be observed that the Type C has a body designed in accordance

with the modern ideas of fairing, or streamlining. Mr. William Heynes, the engineering director of the Jaguar company, expressed to The Autocar the view that this fairing was a very material help in achieving the very high speed of which the cars are capable. He pointed out that the streaks of dust showing on the outside of the body after the race are practically in straight lines along the length of the car, which is an indication that air eddy currents are not being caused.

Although a car of this variety does not need to have much accommodation, the Type C has one or two recesses, notably in the hollow of the door and on the opposite side, also on the right side below the bonnet. The battery is carried below the door, and the tools below the second seat if one is is position. If there is no seat a leather tonneau cover streamlines the opening of the cockpit.

SPECIFICATION

Engine.—6 cylinders 83 × 106 mm (3,442 c.c.). Overhead valves at 70 degrees operated by twin overhead camshafts driven by two-stage Duplex chain. Large valves have Austenitic seats in aluminium alloy detachable cylinder head. Aluminium alloy pistons, steel connecting rods, counterweighted crankshaft in seven 2⅛in steel-backed bearings. Pump water circulation. Full-flow Tecalemit oil filter. Twin horizontal S.U. carburettors. Twin exhaust system. Hemispherical combustion chambers. Compression ratio 8 to 1 for 80 octane fuel, gives 200 b.h.p. at 5,800 r.p.m. 9 to 1 ratio for 85 octane fuel gives 210 b.h.p. at 5,800 r.p.m.

Transmission.—Borg and Beck dry single-plate clutch with solid centre and bonded riveted lining. 4-speed synchromesh gear box with central lever. Overall gear ratios, normal 3.31, 4.51, 6.59, and 11.2 to 1; close ratio box, 3.31, 3.99, 5.78, and 9.86 to 1. Axle ratios available, 2.9, 3.31, 3.54, 3.75, 3.92, 4.09, and 4.27 to 1. Final drive by Hardy Spicer propeller-shaft to hypoid bevel axle with semi-floating shafts.

Suspension.—Independent front with wishbones and torsion bar springs. Special controlled rear with torsion bar springs and torque reaction couplings. Newton hydraulic dampers back and front.

Brakes.—Lockheed hydraulic, 2 L.S. front. Self adjusting. 12in drums.

Steering.—Rack and pinion. Adjustable wheel.

Wheels and Tyres.—Dunlop Road Racing, 6.50 × 16in on knock-off wire wheels with light alloy rims.

Electric Equipment.—Lucas 12 volt, Lucas coil; 40 ampère-hour battery. Champion N.A.10 or N.A.12 sparking plugs.

Fuel System.—40-gallon rear tank; two S.U. electric pumps.

Main Dimensions.—Wheelbase 8ft. Track 4ft 3in. Overall length 13ft 1in, width 5ft 4½in, height (screen down) 3ft 2½in. Ground clearance 5½in. Turning circle 31ft. Dry weight, 18½ cwt approximately.

Ducting over the carburettor intakes matches up with an air intake duct built into the bonnet panelling and taking in fresh air at the front of the car.

The body of the new Jaguar competition car is smooth and functional; the whole of the front panel is hinged at the front and can be pivoted up to give access to the engine compartment and front suspension. A single door is built into the driving side, and to the top of this is attached a plastic extension which follows the line of the curved windscreen.

A STRIKING JAGUAR FOR LE MANS

C-TYPE SUPERSEDED BY A STREAMLINED COMPETITION MODEL

THE latest car to come off the secret list is the new Jaguar competition model which will be seen at Le Mans next month. Not content to rest on their laurels with the sweeping victory that the C-type car gained in last year's 24-hour race the design staff, headed by Mr. W. M. Heynes, has produced a brand new model which will present a very strong challenge to all other competitors. Although it is a completely new car many of the mechanical components are similar to those used previously in Jaguar competition models, but much development work has been done during the winter months.

The most significant changes are in the body style and general layout of the components. To increase maximum speed, using a given power unit, it is necessary to reduce the overall drag, and to achieve this the streamlining must be improved or the frontal area reduced. Both of these items have received attention. The potential performance has been further improved by a substantial reduction in weight, and with the further development which has taken place the power output of the engine, rated at 220 b.h.p. last year, is now believed to be in the order of 250 b.h.p., although no detailed performance figures are at present available.

One of the most impressive things about this car is the extremely low overall height, a mere 32in to the top of the scuttle, 2in lower than last year's car, yet with a satisfactory ground clearance of 7in. From this it might be thought that the driving compartment would be particularly cramped, but from personal experience it can be stated that the layout is extremely comfortable even for a driver who tops the 6ft mark; moreover, the seating has been arranged so that the driver immediately feels at home once he has threaded his legs between the steering wheel and the seat cushion.

Very few technical details have been released as yet, but the engine, which is developed from the C type seen at Le Mans last year, now has dry sump lubrication in order to reduce the overall height

A neat metal cover fits over the passenger compartment and produces a smooth wind-cheating exterior surface on the left side of the body. The twin exhaust pipes protrude through the bottom of the body just in front of the bulkhead and end in front of the rear wheels. Twin rear lights are built into the rear quarters and a light to illuminate a competition number is fitted on the rear panel just above the spare wheel locker.

of the engine compartment, and the centre line of the power unit is inclined at an angle of 8 deg to the vertical; this slight inclination is of no great significance, but gives extra clearance between the engine and frame members. In conjunction with the dry sump arrangement is is of course necessary to use two oil pumps—one pressure and one scavenging pump—and an external oil tank, which is mounted in the engine compartment. A light alloy oil cooler is also incorporated in this system and is placed by the side of the radiator. Three side-draught double choke Weber carburettors are supplied with air from a duct in the front air intake scoop.

To take advantage of the increased engine output together with the reduced drag and reduction in weight the gear ratios have been modified—on last year's car first gear was virtually an emergency low. Most of the suspension details remain unchanged, although the attachment point of the A bracket on the rear axle casing is now placed on the centre line of

the propeller-shaft. On the cars that raced at Le Mans last year this bracket was offset, although it was later changed to the central position.

Dunlop disc brakes are fitted to both front and rear wheels; they are of 12¾in diameter with three pairs of pads per disc at the front and two at the rear. Perforated disc centre-lock wheels are used with three-lug hub caps.

All these well-tried mechanical components are mounted in a streamlined stressed skin body structure fabricated from magnesium alloy, the design producing the maximum rigidity with very low weight. A curved plastic shield deflects the wind over the driver's head. There is also a fairing behind the padded neck rest further to reduce drag. A hinged cover provided in this fairing encloses the quick-action fuel filler cap, and a compartment at the rear houses the spare wheel. The main dimensions are: wheelbase 7ft 6in; front track 4ft 2in; overall length 12ft 10in; width 5ft 5½in.

Right: The smooth frontal appearance and low overall height can be appreciated from this angle. The cold air duct for the carburettors is in the top corner of the main air intake, and metal covers enclose the head lamps.

Left: Mr. W. M. Heynes, technical director of Jaguar Cars, at the wheel of the new competition model.

SUCCESS is a word which has unfortunately more than one meaning in this modern and rather commercial-minded world, and even in racing circles there is some confusion ; there are those who consider that to succeed one must inevitably win, while the opposing school of thought believe that to exceed one's previous best is success indeed. When, however, an organisation with but little previous experience of the trials and tribulations of racing enters the lists with a completely new model—and that designed, developed, and proved during the normal confusion created by launching a new volume-production saloon—one is inclined to stand back a little in admiration for their courage, even if, at the same time, there is a slight feeling that they will certainly need to have the gods on their side. Over all there is the hope that the project will succeed, and when finally the Type C Jaguar helped to write a new page in the long history of the 24 Hours of Le Mans everyone felt that this was real success ; a completely new model from a factory new to racing, and the first event entered produced outright victory as well as a new lap record, and Le Mans is not usually the place where victory and the lap record go to the same make.

Readers will remember that the winning Jaguar, driven by Peter Walker and Peter Whitehead, averaged 93.49 m.p.h. for the 24 hours, while the car driven by Stirling Moss and Jack Fairman took and held the lap record at the speed of 105.24 m.p.h. To many that one sentence contains all that is important about the new Jaguar, but the reasons for its production, the shape the design took, and the troubles to be overcome are of almost as much interest.

One has grown to regard the original XK 120 as an old friend although it is only a relatively short time since it was introduced, and earned the unofficial title of the World's Fastest Production Car. Since then the increasing band of enthusiastic owners have entered their cars in every available event, from small club sprints to Le Mans and the Mille Miglia during 1950. While first place eluded the cars in the two classics, enough was learned to show that only slight improvement in each department was required to make them cars to be feared by all possible opposition, and when an XK 120 circulated at Montlhery for one hour at over 130 m.p.h.—just under the flying mile speed in Belgium—more than one French driver had second thoughts about Talbots and Le Mans. With the object of catering for the small number of owners who wanted the ultimate in performance, and were prepared to do without the luxuries and comforts of the super-fast-touring XK, the competition, or C type, was decided on.

It is, of course, terribly easy to write and to read the expression 'was decided on', but it must be remembered that for most of 1950 the principal preoccupation within the Jaguar factory was getting the new Mark VII saloon into production, and it was in fact with only just over six months left before Le Mans that it was possible for the design staff, under the Technical Director, W. M. Heynes, to clear their offices and get out nice clean sheets of drawing paper and start work. The intention can be stated quite simply—and conforms with what everyone tries to do anyway ; increase power, reduce drag, improve braking, reduce weight, and improve handling.

The increased power was obtained by modifications to the halatory system ; both the exhaust system and the inlet ports getting attention. In addition slight alterations were made to the valve timing. Larger S.U. carburettors were fitted with their inlets breathing from a balance box, which was itself fed by ducting from the front of the car, so that the charge would be denser than could be so were the carburettors inhaling the hot and vitiated air beneath the bonnet. These relatively small changes to a basically good design were enough to raise the power output by approximately 25%, giving figures of 200 and 210 b.h.p. respectively on the alternative compression ratios of 8 : 1 and 9 : 1. It is perhaps worth mentioning—the fact has not received much publicity—that the crankcase of the Type C, although identical to the more normal XK 120, is unusual for the great rigidity achieved in an essentially light casting ; one of the illustrations shows how this has been done by very thorough webbing. The hemispherical combustion chambers have the plug offset laterally, while both turbulence and swirl are controlled by the specially shaped inlet port. The way in which turbulence has been controlled in this engine allows very lean mixtures to be used, and even at maximum power full load the consumption is between 0.5 and 0.53 pints per b.h.p. hour. This figure

GENERAL ARRANGEMENT DRAWINGS

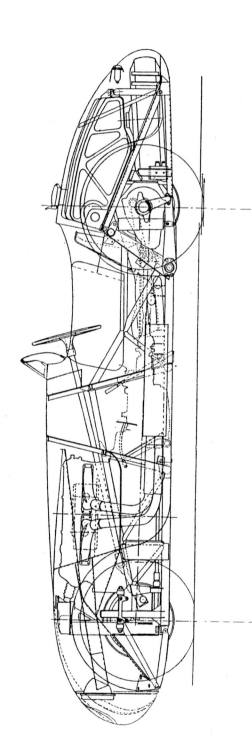

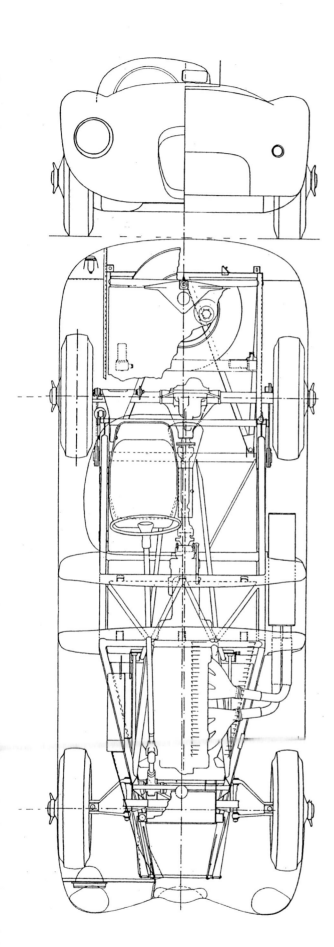

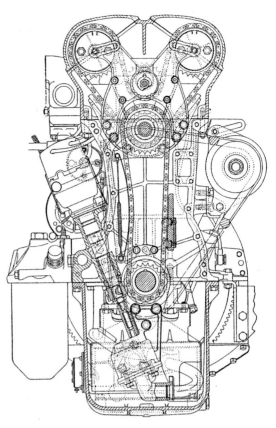

This drawing shows the arrangement of the duplex Renolds chain drive to the overhead camshaft.

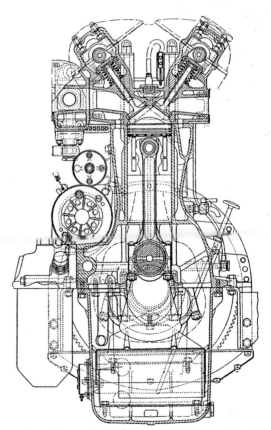

Cross-section of the engine. The internal webbing of the light but rigid crankcase is of particular note.

■ can be compared with the 0.5 pints per b.h.p. hour achieved on the Ricardo-designed Vauxhall 3-litre with a maximum output of only 129 b.h.p., which had been a standard for low-consumption high-efficiency engines. The improvement made to the exhaust system was partially assisted by the new frame design and use of enveloping coachwork. On the XK 120 the exhaust manifold had to be bent sharply down to clear the side members whereas on the Type C there is no appreciable deflecting of the exhausted gas until it has travelled many times the cylinder bore. It is of interest that despite the necessity to reduce drag the expansion chamber was left exposed to the cooling air, with the tail pipes ejecting directly into the air stream.

The body form was improved greatly; to such an extent that 20% less power was required to hold 100 m.p.h. than had been the case with the XK 120. At the same time the practicability of the body was increased by hingeing the bonnet and front assembly complete around the nose, so enabling the engine, all components, and the front suspension to be quickly and easily inspected if necessary during replenishment stops. The reduction in drag allied with the marked increase in maximum power was expected, and such proved to be the case, to raise the maximum speed from around 135 m.p.h. to fractionally under 160 m.p.h. Even during the final development stages it was clear that the new car was a surprising advance on the fast touring version. Although

The type C cylinder head of RR50 aluminium alloy. The curve taken by the inlet ports to control turbulence can be seen.

■ some of the credit must have been due to the much better handling imparted by the new frame and modified suspension an indication of the potentialities of the car was gained when it circulated its proving ground 12% faster than the previous fastest XK 120 could achieve.

Better braking was obtained by utilising a new type of Lockheed hydraulic brake on the front wheels, in which the two leading shoes are self-adjusting. To make certain that the better braking could, if need arose, be used throughout the twenty-four hours, wire wheels were fitted, with central knock-off hubs, which allow much better cooling of the brake drums. There is, too, the added advantage that should a tyre change be necessary minutes can be saved with this type of wheel. The time for a normal pit stop with the winning car varied between 1 min. 44 secs. and 2 mins. 5 secs. and on the tyre change the time taken was only 3 mins. 9 secs., which is almost one-quarter of the time that would be required with the five-stud steel wheels.

The remaining two targets for the design staff—reduction in weight and improvement in high-speed handling and controllability—were in practice closely related. While the chassis is in basis a welded tubular structure, it is assisted by fabricated stiffeners, which act as scuttle and rear bulkhead. As will be seen from the drawing, the entire framework is triangulated, and, in the joint interests of weight-saving and adequate design, the tubing employed has been chosen in relation to the load; the lower and main tubes are of 2 inch, the upper ones $1\frac{1}{2}$ inches, while the connecting struts are 1 inch. The main tubes taper towards the front, where the front suspension wishbones are carried by a cross-braced member. Forward of this a simple framework of channel section carries the tube which supports the hingeing bonnet assembly.

This photograph shows the internal webbing inside the crankcase which gives great rigidity with a considerable saving of weight.

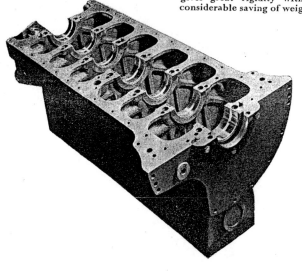

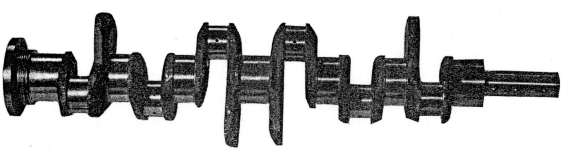

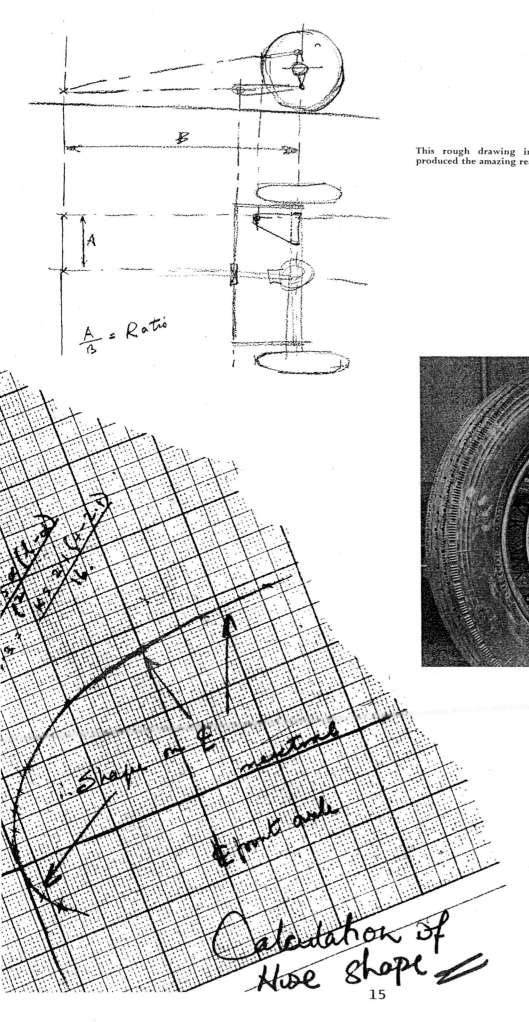

$$\frac{A}{B} = Ratio$$

This rough drawing indicates the principles which produced the amazing rear wheel adhesion of the type C.

Shape of the centre of front axle

Calculation of Hub shape

An intimate view of the front suspension showing the Newton telescopic damper. This photograph was taken in prototype days—hence the standard Dunlop tyres.

Latest Lister-Jaguar with Frank Costin-design body
incorporating a moulded windscreen and high tail

Latest Lister-Jaguar

The 1959 sports-racing car displays, in its clean body design, strong evidence of the teaming of Frank Costin with Brian Lister Ltd. Close attention has been given to cockpit design in the interests of driver comfort. Fuller development to this end envisages full air conditioning. One of these cars will run at Sebring under Briggs Cunningham's entry

ONE of the most interesting sports-racing cars of recent years has been the Lister-Jaguar, notably successful in the hands of the late Archie Scott-Brown. For 1959 no sensational changes to the well-tried chassis design have been made, Brian Lister wisely considering that for the time being at any rate development would largely be restricted to the bodywork and related features, for which his new collaborator, aerodynamicist-structures specialist Frank Costin, assumed responsibility some time ago.

Accompanying this article are pictures of the new sports-racing Lister-Jaguar for the coming season, and it will at once be appreciated that a notable change in appearance has been made for 1959. The car is cleaner-looking and more handsome; and in this instance beauty is more than skin deep. In complimenting the designers and builders on the attractive appearance of the latest Lister we might also commend them on the speed with which they have produced the new car. It was only known a short time ago that Mr. Costin was associating himself with Brian Lister Ltd.; in fact, our announcement of this get-together with great possibilities was only written as we prepared the last number for press. The item had to be held over and appears on page 96; in view of the publication of details of the first fruits of the new team, the paragraph has added interest.

By modern sports-racing car standards the bodywork of the latest Lister-Jaguar is relatively conventional, embodying the results of lessons learnt over the years from previous designs and tests. The moulded screen/high tail arrangement is a logical development of the one originally designed by Mr. Costin for the class-winning Le Mans Lotuses of 1957. This arrangement has since been used by various other manufacturers but it is to be developed further by the Lister team; a tonneau cover, which is the subject of a patent and is essential to the whole conception, for maximum effectiveness, will be added later.

One of the pictures shows that the only bodywork blister is that necessary to accommodate the rather tall Jaguar 3·4-litre engine. This excrescence, however, is made to serve also as a " convection release " of the underbonnet air. For various reasons it was decided not to place the engine on its side at this stage, although it is of dry-sump type.

Ducted radiator not used

In all his earlier designs Mr. Costin has made use of a fully ducted radiator. It is significant to note, therefore, that the new Lister has merely an entry duct. It is possible that further developments may include ducting aft of the radiator. Cold air is taken from the relatively static region to the rear of the front wheel well, over the surface of the oil cooler and thence to the cockpit, the considerable depression in this latter region being responsible for the cooling flow.

The inboard Dunlop disc brakes at the rear are cooled by the method used so successfully on the Vanwall, in which the hot boundary layer of air is scraped from the disc while a considerable volume of cold air is closely ducted around it via a raised intake in the undertray. (Ducts and attachments for this system weigh less than 2 lb., it is worth mentioning.) A duct around the finned rear cover serves to cool the de Dion-type Salisbury final drive unit.

Cockpit and seating

The cockpit, which by any standards is roomy and comfortable, as the relevant picture brings out, is still the subject of detail testing and development but nevertheless represents a noteworthy contribution to driver comfort. In its ultimate form it will be fully air-conditioned, a thought which is both

Striking front view of the car, which will be seen publicly for the first time at the Goodwood Easter meeting. The " power bulge " for the vertical Jaguar engine is also used to release underbonnet air

Latest idea in racing car seating. Foam rubber cushion and squab-surround are supported on Pirelli elastic webbing. Seat frame is tubular steel, the surround trimming is of hide, and the centre panels are in bedford cord

startling and, in the final analysis, logical. Students of motor racing will need no reminding that indifference to cockpit basic ventilation made driving the famous Delage 1½-litre cars of 1926-27 an uncomfortable ordeal; and other excellent cars have been nearly as bad. Why not, therefore, take development to its logical peak in the light of modern knowledge ?

Another contribution to driver comfort on this latest Lister car is the new seating, specially designed by Cox & Co. (Watford) Ltd. These new seats are considered by Listers to be the last word in racing car seating design.

Frontal area is low for a vehicle of this engine capacity and, when coupled with the expected low drag coefficient, should yield maximum speeds in the region of 180 m.p.h. from 250 b.h.p. Equipped with the recently developed 3·8-litre 300 b.h.p. Jaguar engine for British and United States circuits this car should have an interesting performance. It can be had with the 3·4-litre engine and also, for current Appendix C racing, the 3-litre Jaguar unit.

As we have said, chassis details remain, at this stage, virtually unchanged—with one important exception; for 1959 Dunlop disc brakes will be used. Thus, tyres, wheels and brakes on the 1959 Listers are now all made by the same organisation.

"Dick" Barton, Lister's No. 1 racing mechanic, will accompany the cars to all meetings this year, together with a team from the works. Don Moore, who has his own business in Cambridge, will be in charge of the engine side of preparation and maintenance. Drivers for the works cars during 1959 are Ivor Bueb and Bruce Halford. Other drivers may join the team from time to time, particularly for long-distance events such as the Le Mans 24-hours and the Nurburgring 1,000-kilometres races. It is interesting to note that the first of these new Lister-Jaguars has been bought by Mr. Briggs Cunningham and it will run in the Sebring race. All followers of the sport will wish the constructors and users of these promising new cars the best of luck during the coming season.

SPECIFICATION OF LISTER-JAGUAR

The 3½-litre six-cylinder Jaguar engine is too well known to need more than passing reference. With a bore and stroke of 83 mm. and

106 mm. respectively, it has a capacity of 3442 c.c. With a compression ratio of 9 to 1, the maximum b.h.p. is 250 at 6,000 r.p.m. In the Lister, it has three twin-choke Weber carburettors, fed by two S.U. electric fuel pumps.

The tank of the dry sump system holds five gallons and a Tecalemit full-flow oil filter is provided. A Marston Excelsior lightweight radiator is used.

A 3-litre Jaguar engine is also available, this having a bore of 83 mm. and a stroke of 92 mm.; the capacity is 2986 c.c. This can be equipped with the latest 35/40 head at an extra charge. Top power figure is probably in the region of 260 b.h.p., based on last season's performances.

Concerning the transmission arrangements, the clutch is a Borg & Beck three-plate one with six springs; it is hydraulically operated. The four-speed Jaguar gearbox has syncromesh on all gears. The overall ratios are: Top: 3·54 to 1; 3rd: 4·525; 2nd: 5·825; and 1st: 7·610.

The Salisbury final drive unit incorporates hypoid gears. The following eight ratios are available: 2·93, 3·31, 3·54, 3·77, 4·09, 4·27, 4·55 and 4·78 to 1.

The final drive unit incorporates the American Powr-Lok differential unit of the Dyna Corporation of Toledo, but the ZF limited-slip differential, as recently described and illustrated in this journal, is available at an extra charge.

MAIN DIMENSIONS

Wheelbase:	7 ft. 6¾ in.
Track:	4 ft. 4 in. front. 4 ft. 5½ in. rear.
Overall length:	14 ft. 4¾ in.
Overall width:	5 ft. 7 in.
Overall height:	2 ft. 7 in. at scuttle. 3 ft. 2 in. overall.
Ground clearance:	4¼ in. at sump. 6 in. chassis.
Turning circle:	40 ft.
Dry weight:	15½ cwt.
Tank capacity:	38 imperial gallons.

PERFORMANCE DATA

Top gear m.p.h. at 1,000 r.p.m. 24.
Weight distribution dry: 48 per cent front, 52 per cent rear.
A few leading chassis particulars will be of interest.

Construction:	3 in. by 14 gauge seamless drawn steel tube.
Brakes:	Dunlop disc. 12 in. dia. front. 12 in. dia. rear.
Suspension:	Front: Equal length wishbones and coil springs. Rear: de Dion style with coil springs.
Shock absorbers:	Telescopic, Girling manufacture.
Wheels:	Knock-on light alloy 5 in. × 16 in. Perforated disc, Dunlop manufacture.
Tyre size:	Front: 6.00 by 16. Rear: 6.50 by 16 Dunlops.
Steering:	Rack and pinion, with a Derrington light alloy, wood rimmed wheel 15 in. dia. Two turns lock to lock.

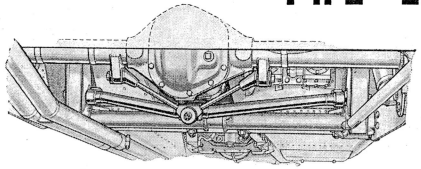

With last year's rear suspension linkage retained, the attachment lugs for the A bracket are now welded to the casing of the live axle

AFTER its very successful début at Le Mans last year when it finished second at an average speed of 105 m.p.h., and subsequently gained first two places in the 12-hour sports car race at Rheims (winning speed 104.55 m.p.h.), it was to be expected that only detail changes would be made to the basic design of the 3½-litre D-type Jaguar. It is interesting to recall that the winning Ferrari at Le Mans recorded a race speed of 105.1 m.p.h. with an engine capacity of 5 litres. The race was run in almost continuous rain, which meant that the brakes were not called upon to the same degree as they would have been had the race been run in the dry. In its turn, this relieved the transmissions of braking loads, and had more normal conditions pertained the result could quite easily have been reversed, as the Ferraris are not renowned for transmission and brake life.

The original D-type Jaguar was quite a departure from the orthodox in chassis and body construction. It used no separate chassis frame as such, but was built around a *monocoque* elliptical centre section extending forward from which, and integral with it, was the front frame section, forming the attachment point for the engine and suspension units. This was constructed of square and round section aluminium tubes welded at their junction points. The tail section, which contained the fuel tanks and spare wheel, was bolted to the rear bulkhead of this centre section. A detailed description of this car was given in *The Autocar* dated September 3, 1954.

Production Version

A considerable demand from private owners resulted from their successful performance at Le Mans and Rheims, and the Jaguar company decided to produce them in quantity for sale to the public; an initial batch of 150 with detail modifications was put in hand.

The major modification was in the frame. The integral construction was found to be expensive in the event of damage, and a separate frame using the same basic tubular type of construction, but with steel tubes, was adopted. To this the main centre section is now bolted. This, as previously, is constructed in magnesium alloy with the stiffening members riveted to the skin. Also as before, the rear bulkhead of this section forms the attachment points for the rear suspension units, and the tail section containing the tanks and spare wheel.

This change in design means that a

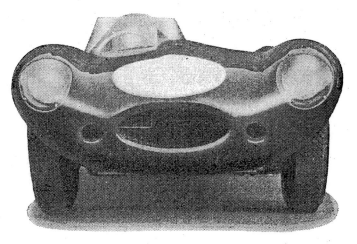

The engine is installed in the chassis at an angle of 8 deg to the right as viewed from the front, which accounts for the bonnet bulge provided to clear the valve gear cover

damaged centre section, or the frame, can be replaced as a separate unit; furthermore, it is a much better production proposition. The main frame, with engine and gear box, and the front suspension, can be built up as one unit. Before being married to it, the centre section can also be treated as a sub-assembly, to be built up with the rear axle and suspension units.

In its aluminium form the chassis frame was welded at all joints. Argon arc welding was used and this is a comparatively costly and slow process. When changing over to the tubular steel frame, welding at the joints was replaced by brazing. Extensive laboratory tests have proved that this results in a much stronger joint with the 45 tons per sq in tubing used; the thickness of tube is 18 s.w.g. for the main structural members and 20 s.w.g. for those not so heavily loaded.

By the use of steel tubes of lighter section, this change has not resulted in any additional weight, and, in fact, the new frame is not as heavy as its aluminium predecessor.

As in all Jaguar competition cars, the power unit is basically the same as the production XK140 engine, retaining the crankshaft, bearing sizes, connecting rods and cylinder block. Dry sump lubrication is used, which requires an additional pump and modified sump. This continued use of the unit speaks very well for the basic design, especially when it is realized that the power output has

been increased to 285 b.h.p. It represents an increase of 35 b.h.p. over last year's car, gained mainly from a modified head, which is under development.

The maximum speed of the engine is limited by its stroke (106 mm) to 6,000 r.p.m., which is a little over 4,000ft per min mean piston speed. To obtain the increase in power without being able to raise the speed range means that the point of peak volumetric efficiency must also be raised. This now occurs at 5,500 r.p.m. when a brake mean effective pressure of 190 lb per sq in is achieved; this indicates excellent breathing capacity when using a compression ratio of 9 to 1.

In conjunction with the increase in engine power, improvements to the body form have also been made which have raised the maximum speed by some 10 m.p.h. This has been achieved by extending the nose section of the body and providing it with a rounded form; at the same time the cooling duct has been placed nearer the ground, and its form modified. Alongside the main entry for radiator air, a separate intake on each side is provided for brake cooling. This improvement has lowered the brake operating temperature by nearly 200 deg F.

The wrapped round windscreen is completely swept into the driver's head rest, the form of which has also been modified. It is now considerably wider at its junction point with the main body form. A degree of wind buffeting was experienced by the drivers in last year's

JAGUAR, 1955

The modified body form, in conjunction with a 14 per cent increase in engine power, has increased the maximum speed by approximately 10 m.p.h.

cars, and this has been reduced to such a degree that the cars can be driven at 150 m.p.h. without the need for goggles. A further detailed modification has been made to the rear suspension, which consists of a live axle and trailing arms with a single transverse torsion bar. Previously the open A bracket for lateral location of the axle was attached by U bolts; these have now been replaced by a bracket welded to the main casing. No change to the geometry of the rear suspension results from this modification.

An oil pump has been introduced for lubrication of the gear box bearings. The normal splash system with wet sump is retained, but the pump has been installed in addition to reduce any possibility of oil starvation to the layshaft and primary shaft bearings. One of Britain's main hopes is, therefore, centred on a car which has been modified in detail and given an increased performance, after making a successful début last year. Its past performances have illustrated the ability to last the full distance of this very arduous race. It was proved in 1953 that brake life plays a very important part in the result and in this respect the Jaguar team, along with many other British competitors, appear to retain a lead over their Continental rivals.

With the 1953 winning combination of Hamilton and Rolt to lead the team of three cars, Jaguars must be well placed among the short odds favourites.

SPECIFICATION

Engine.—6 cyl, 83 mm bore × 106 mm stroke (3,442 c.c.). Compression ratio 9 to 1. 285 b.h.p. at 5,750 r.p.m. Maximum b.m.e.p. 190 lb per sq in at 5,500 r.p.m. Hemispherical head with two valves per cylinder; operated by twin o.h.c.; two-stage chain drive to camshaft; 7 bearing crankshaft with lead bronze bearings. Three 45 mm dia double-choke Weber carburettors. Lucas coil ignition. Champion NA10 sparking plugs.

Transmission.—Borg and Beck dry triple plate clutch 7½in dia. Ball race withdrawal mechanism. Four-speed synchromesh gearbox with pump and splash lubrication. Overall ratios (with 2.53 ratio axle). Top 2.53 to 1, 3rd 3.23, 2nd 4.15, 1st 5.42.

Final Drive.—Hypoid bevel ratio 2.53 to 1. Alternative ratio 2.69 to 1 available. Two-pinion differential.

Suspension.—Front, independent wishbone and torsion bar. Rear, trailing links and torsion bar with live axle. Girling telescopic suspension dampers.

Brakes.—Dunlop disc. Three-pad front; two-pad rear. 12¾in dia. discs front and rear. Total lining area: 75 sq in.

Steering.—Rack and pinion with 16in diameter steering wheel; 1¾ turns from lock to lock.

Wheels and Tyres.—Dunlop light alloy perforated disc, centre lock wheels. 6.50—16in Dunlop racing tyres on 5.00—16in rims.

Fuel and Oil Systems.—37 gallons in two flexible tanks. Dry sump lubrication, tank capacity 3½ gallons.

Electrical Equipment.—12 volt 38 ampère-hour battery. Twin high pressure electric fuel pumps.

Main Dimensions.—Wheelbase, 7ft 6⅜in. Track (front) 4ft 2in, (rear) 4ft 2in. Overall length, 13ft 5⅜in. Width, 5ft 5⅜in. Height at scuttle, 2ft 7½in; at fin, 3ft 9in. Ground clearance, 5¼in under sump. Turning circle, 35ft. Dry weight, 1,940 lb (17 cwt).

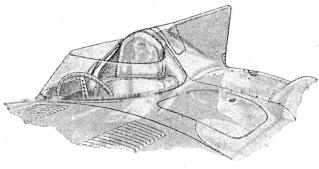

The driver's head rest has been modified to sweep less abruptly into the body. The wrap-round screen blends into the rest

In conjunction with the modified coolant air inlet and extended nose of the body, air tracts to each of the front disc brakes are provided. A considerable drop in brake operating temperature has resulted

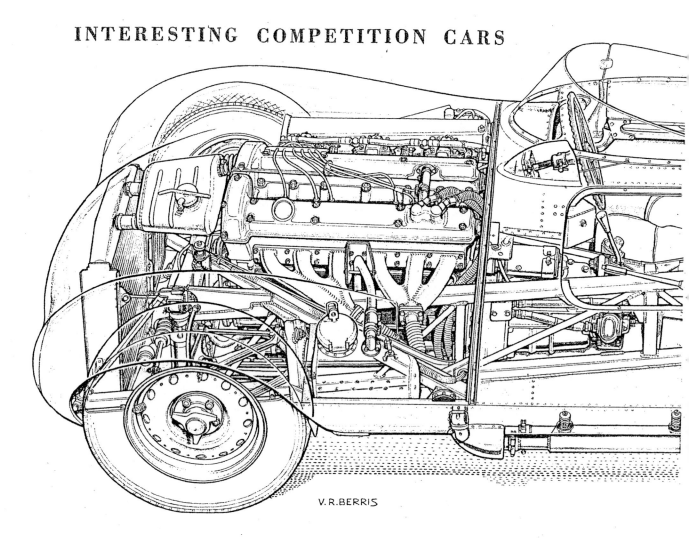

V.R.BERRIS

THE D-TYPE

MONOCOQUE CONSTRUCTION REPLACES

ON the two recent occasions when it has appeared in public, the new competition Jaguar has been extremely successful. At Le Mans in June it gained second and fourth placings, beaten only by the Ferrari powered by a 4,954 c.c. engine, while, soon afterwards at Rheims, it gained the first two places in the 12-hour Sports Car Race. The race averages were 105 m.p.h. at Le Mans (the winning Ferrari recorded 105.1 m.p.h.), and 104.55 m.p.h. at Rheims. So much for its performance, but what of the car itself?

How does it compare with previous competition Jaguars; for example, the cars that gained first, second and fourth positions in the Le Mans 24-hour Race of 1953? The current car is in the direct line of descent from previous models, although there are a number of important differences, outlined in the brief description in *The Autocar* of May 7, 1954.

There are at least two ways of improving a given car's performance: by obtaining greater power from the engine, and by reducing the resistance to motion. The first method increases the amount of work required from the mechanical components; the second can make their task less severe—both approaches have been exploited in the D-type Jaguar.

The C-type Jaguar was built around a tubular frame, the main frame members taking the stresses, while the body panels played a relatively small part in providing structural rigidity. For the D-type, the design of the chassis has been completely revised; there is no separate chassis as such, but the car is built around what may be called a centre-section of monocoque construction and immense strength. This provides a very rigid structure and also results in a useful weight reduction.

The Main Structure

To obtain a clear picture of how the body structure is designed, it is perhaps easiest to consider it as three sections; the centre portion, forming the basis of the structure; the front section, integral with the centre section and housing the engine and front suspension; and the tail assembly (containing the fuel tanks and spare wheel), which is bolted to the centre section.

The centre section consists of an elliptically shaped tube in which are cut suitable openings for the driver and passenger. Below the major axis of the ellipse, extra stiffening is provided by massive L-section pressings, riveted to the main section so that they form, in effect, two tubular members, approximately triangular in cross-section. Both ends of the centre assembly are enclosed by diaphragms which form the front and rear bulkheads.

At the front, a large box-section member is provided above the major axis of the ellipse by the use of two diaphragms and a lower closing plate. In the front bulkhead a central opening houses the transmission and provides additional space for the driver's legs.

The rear bulkhead requires only a small opening, for the propeller-shaft. The good torsional rigidity and beam strength of the centre section is also increased by four tubular members which extend diagonally forward and are welded to the front cross-member. These tubes embrace the complete power unit, while further stiffening is provided by two additional square-section tubes which

20

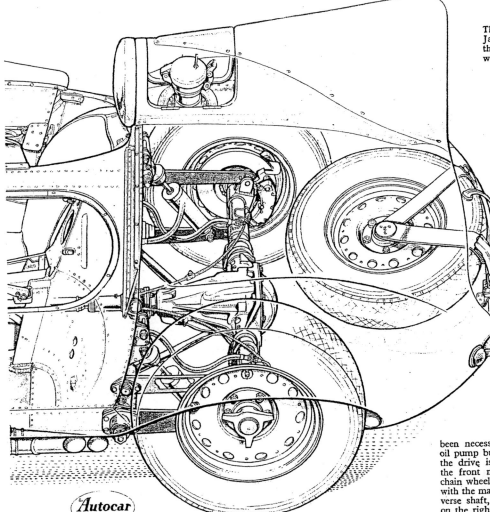

This drawing of the D-type Jaguar shows the layout of the major components together with the main structural members.

JAGUAR

TUBULAR FRAME

run forward diagonally from the front of the bulkhead to meet in the centre of the front cross-member frame. They pass over, and are welded to, the two upper main frame tubes. The whole of the body structure is riveted and arc welded from magnesium alloy, the skin being of 18 gauge material.

Two transverse box-section members are secured to the rear diaphragm, and to these are attached massive vertical assemblies, each of two vertical plates riveted to a channel-section spacer, the whole forming box-section members housing the bearings of the trailing-link rear suspension.

The rear section of the body, which does not carry the main loads, is attached to the centre section by bolts around the periphery of the ellipse, while four additional bolts secure the rear assembly frame members to the rear suspension housing assemblies.

Although the D-type Jaguar is a completely new car, as many standard components as posible are utilized. For example, although the power unit has dry sump lubrication and develops more power than the standard XK 120 power unit, standard production castings are used for both block and cylinder head —a fact which speaks well for the basic design and layout of the engine and demonstrates to the owner of the normal production machine that his power unit is by no means operating near to the bone!

Developments in the XK 120 engine were outlined in some detail in the April 24, 1953, issue of The Autocar. It is, therefore, intended to explain quite briefly some of the subsequent modifications. All details of modifications are not at present available, for, with any competition machine, detailed development continues until it is superseded by a later model.

Engine Details

A single iron casting forms the cylinder block and crankcase, and the bores (which are relatively long, with a bore to stroke ratio of 0.778 to 1), are machined direct in the casting. The general layout of the crankcase is simple, and there is ample structural rigidity, produced by the internal webbing and the arrangement of the housings for the seven main bearings. The crankshaft and big-end bearings are of indium-coated lead-bronze bearings,

and the shaft itself is of EN16 steel.

The engine has no flywheel, but there is a substantial crankshaft torsional vibration damper at the front, and flywheel effect is produced by the mass of the triple dry-plate clutch and its housing, together with the starter ring which is pressed on the clutch assembly centre section.

The most noticeable difference in the appearance of the engine is caused by the change from wet to dry sump lubrication, made to reduce the height of the engine, the sump height having been halved. This not only enables the bonnet line to be lowered considerably without adversely affecting ground clearance, but also lowers the centre of gravity of one of the major masses.

It has, of course, been necessary to provide an additional oil pump but, as on the standard engine, the drive is taken from a gear between the front main bearing and the timing chain wheel. The crankshaft gear engages with the mating gear which drives a transverse shaft, operating the pressure pump on the right-hand side of the engine and the scavenge pump on the left-hand side.

Oil from the tank is drawn by the pressure pump and directed to the bottom of the oil cooler. Forced through the cooler, it passes along an external pipe to the crankcase where it lubricates the bearings via internal drillings in the normal way. Falling to the base of the sump, the oil is returned to the tank by a dual scavenge pump. It is, of course, necessary to make provision for rapid return of the oil to the tank to prevent build-up of lubricant at the base of the engine, and it must also be remembered that oil produces more resistance than air to crankshaft webs rotating at high speed.

With dry sump lubrication, one of the main problems is to prevent aeration of the lubricant, and on the Jaguar engine this has been accomplished by baffles inside the oil tank, with a breather pipe from the top of the tank connected to the crankcase.

As with the production engine, a light alloy cylinder head is used, with valve seat inserts for both inlet and exhaust valves. It has hemispherical combustion chambers and inclined valves, and the engine operates on a compression ratio of 9 to 1. To aid installation, the engine is inclined in the chassis at an angle of 8 deg to the left when viewed from the cockpit. The barrels of the three double-choke Weber carburettors are set at a similar angle to the vertical centre line of the engine, so that they are truly horizontal when the unit is installed. Six

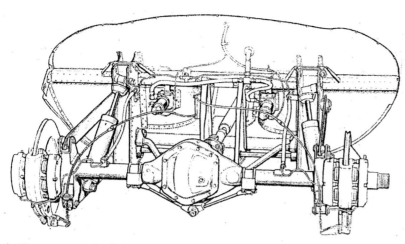

The rear suspension is by means of trailing links and a one-piece torsion bar which is anchored at the centre. Note the disc brakes and additional caliper hand brakes at each end of the axle.

tubular intake ducts are attached to the carburettor intake flanges, and connected by a large-diameter balance tube, the side walls of the intake tubes being cross-drilled at the appropriate points.

An intake duct in the bonnet conveys air from the radiator grille to an open-ended box which, surrounding the carburettor intakes, eliminates the need for pressure balancing pipes to the float chambers. The two three-branch, welded exhaust manifolds direct the gases via two short, flexible pipes into the two main outlet pipes. Just before the pipes terminate in front of the left-hand-side rear wheel, they are enclosed in a sheet-metal cover somewhat similar to a small silencer, which, in conjunction with drilled holes in

the inner walls of the pipes, forms an effective expansion chamber and provides substantial mounting points for securing to the main body structure.

An orthodox arrangement of engine cooling is adopted, but to enable the bonnet height to be kept low a separate light alloy radiator header tank is placed between the front of the engine and the radiator. After passing through the head the coolant is conveyed to the tank which contains outlet pipes at each side, with a central, longitudinal baffle. The intake pipe discharges the coolant near the centre in order to feed both outlets equally and to prevent ineffective cooling that might be caused by the coolant being directed to one side of the radiator.

Both oil and coolant radiators are of light alloy and produced by Marston Excelsior. The radiator system is pressurized to 4lb per sq in by means of a valve unit mounted in the back of the tank.

A conventional fuel system is used, but an unusual feature is the use of flexible tanks, supported in light alloy boxes. To obtain the desired range between refuelling stops, two tanks are used. Twin petrol pumps, placed behind the rear diaphragm, connect to a common delivery pipe to the carburettors.

Power is transmitted from the engine via the triple-plate clutch to the four-speed synchromesh gear box. The main clutch body contains three sets of internal splines equally spaced around its bore, mating with the external splines on the two intermediate driving plates. The rear clutch driven plate is attached to a centrepiece which is internally splined to mate with the gear box input shaft, and contains three sets of external splines carrying the first and second driven plates.

The pressure plate assembly, bolted to the rear, contains six springs together with the toggle levers, which are operated by the ball-bearing thrust withdrawal mechanism. The actual clutch operation is hydraulic by a Girling unit. Radial holes are drilled in the clutch body, to assist cooling and allow lining dust to escape. The complete clutch assembly is housed in a conventional bell housing, with an opening at the back for the starter motor, which is above the transmission on the engine centre line.

Single helical gears are used in the gear box and special close ratios have been chosen. The gears are selected by a short change lever conveniently placed

THE D-TYPE

With the bonnet open the engine and front suspension are very accessible. The oil tank is carried just behind the left front wheel, while the small battery is placed in a similar position behind the right wheel. The large pipe running from the oil tank between the two exhaust manifolds is a breather which is connected to the engine.

The D-type engine can be distinguished by the very shallow sump used in conjunction with the dry sump lubrication system. The torsional vibration damper can be seen at the front of the engine behind the dynamo and water pump driving belts.

just aft of the gear box unit. A small, flexible breather pipe extends forward and upward to the front of the main bulkhead.

From the rear of the gear box, a short Hardy Spicer propeller shaft continues the drive to the Salisbury rear axle. Except for a change in ratio and modified length of the axle tubes, this unit is similar to that fitted in the production XK. It has a hypoid final drive with a ratio of 2.79 to 1 and, with the tyres

JAGUAR .. continued

used at Le Mans, this gives a speed of 183 m.p.h. at 6,000 r.p.m. engine speed.

The front suspension is by upper and lower wishbones and longitudinal torsion bars. The inner fulcrum bearings are in line with the longitudinal centre line of the chassis, and rubber bushes form both upper and lower bearings; the front bushes are conical, while the rear ones are parallel. The upper wishbone—a one-piece forging—contains the ball housing at its outer end to permit the required movement for suspension and steering, while at the inner end there are two split bosses with pinch bolts.

The front boss is threaded internally, while a smaller diameter, plain section is provided for the rear one, the shaft which forms the top wishbone inner fulcrum having screwed and plain portions to mate

with the wishbone. These two portions are concentric with the axis of the shaft, but the portions which pivot in the rubber bushes are eccentric, and the combined effect of the screw thread and eccentricity enables the wheel caster and camber to be adjusted after assembly.

With a number of torsion bar front suspensions, the bar supporting the weight of the car is concentric with the lower pivot point, but in the Jaguar layout, the front member of the lower wishbone assembly extends from its fulcrum point towards the centre of the car, forming a splined attachment for the bar which runs at an angle of 2½ deg to the centre line of the car. This enables the bar to be changed without disturbing the main suspension components, but it also means that the suspension characteristics are modified slightly by the combined effects of bending and torsion. To adjust the height of the car, a vernier arrangement of splines is provided.

Rack and Pinion Steering

The steering arms, extending in front of the wheel centre line, are linked to the rack and pinion steering unit, which is placed fairly high in front of the main cross-member assembly. There is a universal joint in the steering column.

At the rear, the suspension consists of a live axle, trailing arms and a torsion bar. Two massive, box-section members attached to the main body structure pro-

vide bearing housings for the trailing-link units. The top links are 16in long and of flat steel plate of approximately 2 × ½in section. Rubber bushes are used for both the inner and the outer bearings. Metal bushes used for the lower bearings are 1¼in diameter, and are lubricated by grease nipples. Steel plates are also used for the lower links, and these have a similar centre distance to those above, so that a true parallelogram is formed. To provide attachment of the lower links to the torsion bars, bearing units are riveted to the inner ends of the lower links; these are also bored to provide clearance for the torsion bar, and contain a larger diameter outer ring which is internally splined. The ends of the torsion bar, also splined, are of a much smaller diameter, so that, to connect the torsion bar to the rear links, rings are used which are externally splined to mate with the lower links and internally splined to connect with the torsion bar.

The single torsion bar used for the rear suspension has an enlarged centre section which is attached to a reaction plate bolted to the centre of the main body structure and containing arms which pass on each

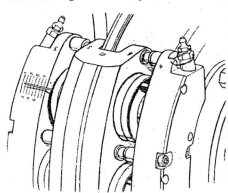

To enable the rate of wear of the brake friction pads to be determined during a race, a small visual indicator is provided with a pointer which lines up with a series of marks engraved on one of the caliper housings.

side of the propeller-shaft. The effective length from the reaction point to the splines is 20in. Under cornering conditions, the plates forming the suspension links are in torsion, increasing the roll stiffness of the car and necessitating the use of material for the links which will permit some flexibility.

To provide transverse location of the axle unit, an open A bracket is pivoted to the main structural members, the bearings being slightly forward of the link bearing line, while the apex of the A

How the tubular frame members are united with the rear diaphragm plate. To provide extra clearance for the driver, a small diameter tube is used in place of a large square section one for the top right-hand member.

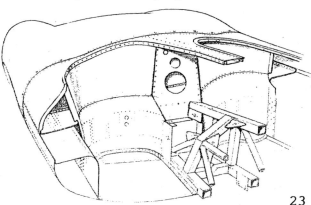

This sketch gives a diagrammatic representation of the main members which form the structure of the car; this complete magnesium-alloy structure has been carefully stressed to provide maximum rigidity with very light weight.

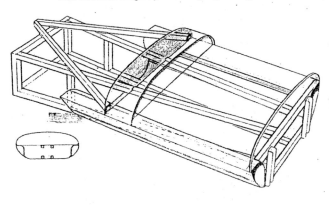

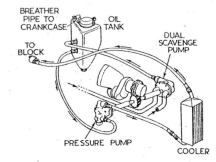

Engine lubrication : A cross shaft, gear driven from the front end of the crankshaft, provides the drive for the pressure and scavenge pumps.

attached to the lower link and bracketed to the main body structure. Built-in bump stops in the dampers consist of large rubber pads placed around the main damper spindle, which contact with the top of the main damper casing, while hydraulic rebound stops are also incorporated.

It was emphasized previously that one of the methods used to improve the performance of the new D-type car was to reduce wind resistance. When the drag of a car is reduced, so that it requires a relatively small b.h.p. to propel it at a high speed, it also requires extremely good brakes, since the retarding effect of air resistance has been reduced. As on last

caliper, machined from medium carbon steel, attached to a suitable flange on the front or rear suspension in the same way as the brake back plate is fixed on a drum-brake system. Bores in this caliper provide housings for the brake pads—which are circular blocks of brake lining material—so that torque reaction is taken by the caliper housing.

To eliminate the effect of disc distortion which might arise through deflection of the rear axle half-shafts when cornering, the rear brake pads are placed symmetrically about the horizontal axis of the wheel centre line. The brake discs are of mild steel, which is hard chromium plated to reduce the rate of wear.

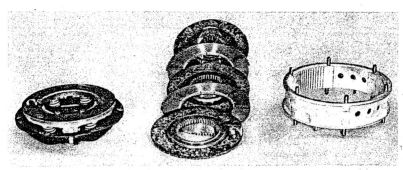

To transmit the drive a neat and compact triple plate clutch is used, and the two intermediate driving plates are splined into the centre portion of the clutch housing.

THE D-TYPE

Under very arduous conditions, the temperature rise in and around the caliper area might cause the brake fluid to boil. To provide adequate cooling, the brake-operating cylinders—one for each pad, twenty cylinders therefore, being required—are arranged in the form of light alloy blocks, attached to the calipers by bolts and distance pieces to provide adequate air space. The outer end of each piston has a spherical seating so that slight tilting of the brake pad does not produce severe side loading on the piston. A normal type of rubber diaphragm seal is fitted towards the outer end of the piston to prevent foreign matter from reaching the cylinder bores. Drillings in the light alloy block take the supply pipes, while nipples are provided at convenient points to enable the system to be bled.

Automatic Adjustment

It is necessary to reduce to a minimum the movement required to bring the brake pads into contact with the disc, but at the same time to ensure that the pads are not rubbing when the brakes are not applied. If an unnecessarily large clearance were provided between pad and disc there would be an excessively long pedal movement before the brakes came into operation, owing to the large number of operating cylinders that are employed in this system.

To overcome this difficulty an ingenious system of retraction and automatic adjustment is provided to maintain

terminates in a bearing which is secured by a bracket to the axle tubes, serving not only to provide transverse location but also to determine the height of the rear roll centre.

The suspension is damped by CDR 4½ type Girling telescopic dampers. At the front these are attached to the upper section of the front cross member at the top and the lower wishbone at the bottom, while the rear dampers are inclined transversely to clear the upper suspension links, the damper itself being

year's cars, Dunlop disc brakes are fitted to all four wheels. They have 12¾in diameter discs and three pairs of pads are used at the front, and two at the rear, to provide the required braking distribution. All the pads are 2³⁄₁₆in diameter, so that the total friction lining area for the foot brake is 45 sq in front and 30 sq in rear. To improve the brake life, the volume of the friction material has been increased by approximately 20 per cent since last year.

Structurally, the brakes consist of a

Left: Air scoops form part of the unsprung mass on the front suspension, and direct air over the front brake discs.

The front torsion bars are attached to an extension on the front portion of the lower wishbone, which is continued in past the fulcrum point.

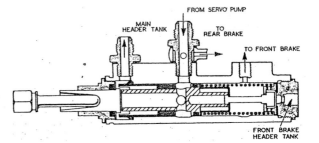

only 0.010in to 0.015in clearance between the pad and the disc when the brakes are in the off position.

To apply the brakes, a dual hydraulic system is provided, with servo assistance by a Plessey pump driven, from the back end of the gear box, whenever the propeller-shaft is rotating. A simple hydraulic layout is used to operate the front brakes which, if necessary, can be applied without assistance from the servo, in the event of a failure occurring in the servo circuit.

With the servo in operation, the fluid is pumped from the header tank into the rear of the master cylinder, through four cross drillings into the hollow centre-

The layout of the pistons in the brake master cylinder. An hydraulic servo is used.

JAGUAR .. continued

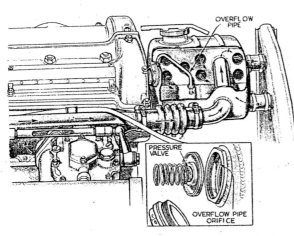

A baffle plate is fitted halfway across the radiator header tank to distribute the flow through both sides of the film block. The overflow pipe from the pressure valve runs out through the base of the header tank.

section of the rear portion of the piston, and out into another pipe which returns to the header tank. Whenever the car is in forward motion the fluid circulates in this way.

When the brakes are applied, the rear piston is forced against the main piston, applying the front brakes, and at the same time preventing the fluid from the servo pump returning to the header tank. The line pressure from the servo pump increases, and as this pipe is connected to the rear brakes they also are applied, and at the same time the build-up in servo pressure exerts a force on the back

of the master cylinder piston which applies the front brakes.

Although it is necessary for the driver's foot to close the valve which increases the line pressure, the area so covered is much less than the area of the front brake master cylinder piston, and it is this difference which determines the servo ratio.

As the servo pump is driven from the output side of the propeller-shaft, it will be rotated in reverse whenever the car moves backward, and, unless precautions were taken, this might cause air to be drawn into the system.

A valve box is fitted between the input and output pipes from the pump, with a non-return valve so placed that pressure in the suction side of the pump causes the valve to open, providing a short open circuit between inlet and outlet sides of the pump. Two separate sets of mechanically operated calipers with triangular friction linings, fitted below the main hydraulically operated units on the rear brakes, are operated by a single cable connected to the handbrake lever by a pulley compensating mechanism.

To reduce weight, perforated disc light alloy wheels are used. They have a centre-lock fixing but, in place of the splined hub often used on a conventional centre-lock wheel, the wheel disc is attached to a steel centre portion by five bolts which have domed heads. These locate in holes drilled in the back flange of the hub and transmit drive or braking torque.

The cockpit is well laid out and is free from unnecessary equipment. It contains three instruments—a tachometer with an additional hand to record the maximum speed which the engine attains, an oil pressure gauge and a water temperature gauge. The steering wheel is adjustable and held on its splined column by a screwed clamp. In true racing tradition it has light alloy spokes and a neat wooden rim.

The curved plastic windscreen sweeps well round the sides of the cockpit, and the rear part of the body has a head rest just in front of the fuel filler cap and, to improve the direction stability under adverse wind

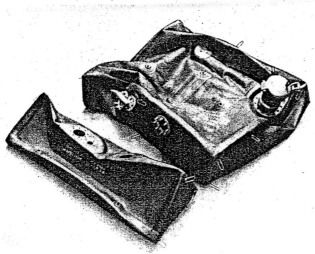

The fuel is carried in two flexible tanks which are neatly fitted into light alloy boxes in the tail of the car.

conditions, particularly at speeds of over 150 m.p.h., a tail fin which neatly blends into the driver's head rest.

SPECIFICATION

Engine.—6-cyl. 83 × 106 mm, 3,442 c.c. Compression ratio 9 to 1. 250 b.h.p. at 6,000 r.p.m. Maximum torque 242 lb ft at 4,000 r.p.m. Seven-bearing crankshaft. Hemispherical combustion chambers. Overhead valves operated by twin overhead camshafts.

Clutch.—Three plates, six springs. Hydraulically operated, ball-bearing withdrawal mechanism.

Gear Box.—Ratios: Top 2.79; third 3.57; second 4.58; first 5.98 to 1. Reverse 6.1 to 1.

Final Drive.—Hypoid bevel, ratio 2.79 to 1 (14:39). Two-pinion differential.

Suspension.—Front, independent, wishbone and torsion bars. Rear, trailing link and torsion bar. Suspension rate (at the wheel) front, 120 lb per in; rear, 120 lb per in.

Brakes.—Dunlop disc. Three-pad front; two-pad rear. Discs: front 12¾in diameter,

The starter ring is attached to the centre of the clutch casing; no normal flywheel is used, the necessary flywheel effect being obtained by the mass of the clutch and ring.

rear 12¾in diameter. Total lining area: 75 sq in; 45 sq in front.

Steering.—Rack and pinion. Eight-toothed pinion. 1¾ turns from lock to lock.

Wheels and Tyres.—Dunlop light alloy, perforated disc, centre-lock wheels. 6.50-16in Dunlop racing tyres on 5.00-16in rims.

Electrical Equipment.—12-volt; 40-ampère-hour battery. Head lamps, 48- or 60-watt bulbs.

Fuel and Oil System.—37 Imp. gallons in two flexible tanks. Oil capacity 3½ gallons.

Main Dimensions.—Wheelbase 7ft 6in; track (front) 4ft 2in; (rear) 4ft. Overall length 12ft 10in. Width 5ft 5¼in. Height, at scuttle, 2ft 8in; at fin, 3ft 8in. Ground clearance 5½in under sump. Frontal area 10.85 sq ft. Turning circle 32ft.

Pile-up at Club Corner, Silverstone 1956, during the "Daily Express" Trophy Race. "E.E.'s" Jaguar No. 9, Sanderson; Aston Martin, No. 23, of Salvadori; "Works" Jaguar, No. 3, of Titterington.

RACING WITH JAGUAR & ECURIE ECOSSE

RON GAUDION CONTINUES HIS STORY OF THE 1955-56-57 SEASONS.

Australian, Ron Gaudion, now with B.P. Australia as an automotive lubricants representative, continues the story of the three seasons he spent, firstly in the Competition Dept. of Jaguar Cars Ltd. and later with Ecurie Ecosse. In last months magazine he finished with Le Mans '56 when the E.E. Jaguar won.

Then followed a very enjoyable drive up to Sweden for the Grand Prix, where we had two cars entered, but, unfortunately, at approximately half distance Flockhart had lost oil pressure through a broken delivery pipe and made a spectacular "Blow Up" in front of the stands overtaking another car up the pit straight. Sanderson retired with back-end trouble.

Oulton Park then finished the '56 season for us.

Mille Miglia

The first race of the 1957 season was the Mille Miglia which entailed a very picturesque drive through France over the Mt. Ceris Pass into Italy to Brescia, via Turin.

This race of 1000 miles through or around Italy, over mountains and plains alike, is road racing at its best, but unfortunately, extremely dangerous for drivers and spectators alike.

De Portargo, who unfortunately lost a rear wheel nearing the finish, somersaulted doing approx. 150 m.p.h., killing himself, co-pilot Nelson and eleven spectators.

Our car, with Flockhart driving solo, lasted approximately 500 miles, the half way mark, then suffered a fractured tail section and retired.

Then up to Nurburgring in Germany, with three cars entered in the 1000 kilometre race. The usual hive of industry takes place at each circuit a week before the event, preparing and repairing cars which perhaps suffered in the last event hundreds of miles away, yet unloaded, worked on, tested and raced again.

After repairing the Mille Miglia car and preparing the other two we took the private team prize by all cars finishing fairly well up.

Next came St. Etienne in Vichy, France, to take a 1st and 2nd.

To add to our many experiences, we had to "make do" with very limited daily expenses. Many a time as we travelled we economised by cooking a home-made do-it-yourself meal in order to have a night or two out in our favourite haunts.

Different currencies can cause headaches, especially when passing through two or three countries in a day, or as many as seven in a week. And there were customs controls, too, at each border, where cars, transporters, spares, etc., etc., had to be passed and checked before we could proceed.

Languages play a big part, but it's amazing how useful your hands prove to be at a time like this, for explaining things, although sometimes, "dumb stupidity" can be the best policy.

Now came a slice of real success. From St. Etienne we drove back through France to Le Mans. This time we had two car entered, only to manage a repeat performance of the year before and also a 2nd.

Faced with our biggest opposition from the most powerful sports cars ever built by Ferrari and Maserati, we completely outpaced them to finish 1st and 2nd.

Incidentally the first driver to break a 4-minute lap time and do the magic 200 k.p.h. lap was Mike Hawthorn in a 4.1 Ferrari.

Thus two privately entered cars won the most publicised and the longest sports car race in the world. Even a team with the full backing of the works behind it, could scarcely have hoped to do better — few manufacturer's teams could hope even to equal it.

The following week-end was to find us at Monza. To get there from Le Mans meant loading up both transporters directly after the race, so as to get an early start on the Monday morning, as we were to reach Monza Wednesday evening. Needless to say all aboard after breakfast, but the green transporter moved only 100 yards then squealed to a halt. The rear offside spring had broken.

This entailed many hours of work to remove, repair and replace, with the air blue and moods to match. We eventually got mobile at 11.30 p.m. that night and there followed a nightmare trip through France to the Mediterranean and around the Riviera, due to the short-cut across the Alps being blocked with snow and washed out roads. We passed through Marseilles, Monte Carlo, Nice and so on to Genoa and Monza, arriving Wednesday afternoon, two days and three blow-outs later. Traffic and border control hold ups, too,

RACING WITH JAGUAR AND E.E.

left us very frustrated and short tempered.

Mr. Murray, who had arrived before us with the drivers, was anxiously waiting for our safe arrival, and as ever, was very thoughtful in warning the hotel staff to have warm baths, a good meal and beds ready for us.

The Monza 500-mile race was run in three heats of 167 miles each on the Autodroma, an oval concrete track with a straight each side and a wall, saucer-shaped, each end-banking.

This "Cup of the two Worlds" has been the most controversial race since the war. The U.S.A. drivers were very disappointed indeed at the non-appearance of the European drivers. Only Borniggia with a 4.1 Ferrari and Jean Behra with a 3.5 Maserati were interested enough beside the Ecurie Ecosse team of three cars, But, unfortunately, Borniggia failed to qualify at the required 145 m.p.h. lapping of the circuit, and Jean Behra had the misfortune to blow up his Masser.

The arrival of our equipe made a very good impression and were warmly welcomed, although outclassed and treated as amateur motorists, by the U.S.A. teams with their ponderous Indianapolis Specials. These were painted bright colours, with advertisements plastered hither and thither, list of driver, owner and mechanics names printed on each side, also the name of the particular 'equipe or Special over the top of the bonnet and tail.

Mechanics proudly wore their names on the pocket of overalls and that of the Equipe, etc., on the back in big letters, cigars hanging from their mouths, in some cases 10-gallon hats (Texan contingent).

They reminded me very much of Wirth's Circus coming to town.

What with their wheel-balancing plant and hoist brought over from Indianapolis and re-erected in the paddock at Monza, I'm quite sure the local Italian people thought the Yanks were all set to let off either the "Explorer" or "Vanguard" rocket.

We spent Thursday stripping all three cars of head and tail lamps, starter motors, dynamos — in fact, everything that could be removed to reduce weight — and adding temporary air scoops to front and rear to help keep the tyres cool under the very arduous conditions. The temperature was 104°F. in the shade.

After the first practice the Americans had difficulty with their suspensions — shockers were going left, right and centre — also frames cracking and fuel tanks splitting. Yes, the American teams were worried. They feared the pounding of the concrete banking; and rightly so, since a little over two hours practice had played such havoc with them.

Of the ten cars, six had Kurtis Kraft frames, two Kwyma's, one Phillip and one John Zink.

The two Novi's had V8 twin o.h.c. 2.8-litre engines with centrifugal supercharged aero carburettors. Developing 580 b.h.p. at 7,500 r.p.m., they cost in the region of £40,000 to build. The remainder were Offenhauser-Meyer-Drake twin o.h.c. 4-cylinder 4.2-litre with fuel injection developing 400 b.h.p. Chassis features were independent suspension on transverse torsion bars, front trailing links with line rear axle, two speed gear boxes, disc-brakes, and the engine offset to left. They used plastic or fibreglass coated fuel tanks.

Their approximate weight was 16 cwts. They had fierce-looking air intake tubes as big as motor horns, and Firestone tyres 8.00 x 20 were fitted.

The Jaguars were two 3.5-litre, and one 3.8-litre with fuel injection developing approximately 295 b.h.p. In fact they were the same two cars that had raced less than a week before and finished 1st and 2nd in the 24-Hour, and they were raced without engines being touched, other than the fitting of harder plugs and bigger jets. We were limited to small wheels by the overhanging sports body. Dunlop 6.50 x 16 were used, with 3 m.m. of tread on the near side wheels and 5 m.m. on the offside. We had been warned by the experts, not to exceed 150 m.p.h. as the treads could not stand the centrifugal force and track pounding.

A rolling start was used to suit the American cars as they had only two gears. On the first lap, Fairman, making full use of his 4-speed box, simply left the pack for dead

and shot away to pass the pits well in the lead, while the crowd, and E.E. included, came to their feet, roaring with delight and amazement; but the U.S.A. drivers soon got their faster machinery rolling and passed at will.

An amusing incident was when Troy Ruttman accelerated away from the pits after a refuel, still holding a drink in paper cup and throwing it away just before entering the first banking. Another was Jimmy Bryan sucking a cigar right through the race.

Pit signals were rather unique, holding out a boot for instance (faster) or showing so many fingers of either hand or both. How a driver could distinguish this signal passing at 170 m.p.h. beats me.

Fairman is a very keen and enthusiastic driver, who will drive to instructions implicitly. He gained the nick name "Fearless Jock" at Monza, as the only driver to get right on top of the banking. He climbed far higher than anyone else, so high in fact, that he removed one bonnet strap and stripped the paint to the metal through touching the safety fence at the top. Never flustered, he always took his time in preparing his helmet, gloves, scarf, etc., and gained "Flash Jock" as another nickname.

Gradually, as the race wore on, cars were shaken apart. Between heats pit crews slaved at repairing damage to frames and suspension with oxy torches, and fitting new shockers. Near-panic prevailed among the other teams, wondering if they would suffer likewise, while the three Jaguars quenched their thirst with oil topup and fuel replenishment.

Myself, and many others I might add, felt that had the race been continuous for the 500 miles the Jaguars would almost certainly have won it.

For the last heat, only four U.S.A. cars remained, Jim Bryan, Troy Ruttman, John Parsons and Pat O'Connor, but unfortunately, O'Connor failed to finish. Jim Bryan won by 5½ miles at a race average of 160 m.p.h., and also fastest lap time of 175.7 m.p.h. Ruttman was 2nd, Parsons 3rd, and Fairman, Lawrence and Sanderson 4, 5 and 6 respectively, this 4-5-6 performance added greatly to the prestige of Ecurie Ecosse.

After returning to Edinburgh, we raced one car at Silverstone (Le Mans winner 3.8), then did the Swedish Grand Prix. On our return journey we concluded the 1957 season at Spa in Belgium.

Then we settled down for our winter "Liberation", rebuilding all the cars and constructing a new Lister-Jaguar early this year! This was completed shortly before my return to Melbourne last April.

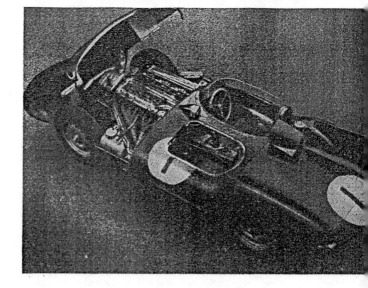

On the two occasions they have appeared in competition this year the new Jaguar "D" Types have been successful. At Le Mans they ran second and fourth and in the Rheims 12 Hour Race first and second. The performance of the car is good, to say the least. At Le Mans it was geared down to give it a top speed of just on 183 m.p.h., with acceleration from 0 to 100 m.p.h. being in the order of about 15 seconds. So much for the performance of the car; what are the main differences between this car and its predecessor, the "C" type, which also achieved successes in international competition.

Chiefly, the differences are these; monococque construction is used on the

Stressed-skin Chassis for new Jaguar "D"

type "D", instead of using a chassis the stressed skin principle is used. The body-chassis may be divided up into two separate parts, the engine and passenger compartments and the rear of the shell, this latter part bolts on to the front making the whole extremely rigid. This type of construction also cuts down body weight considerably. Aerodynamics have also been improved and the addition of a stabilising fin, set up just behind the driver's headrest improves directional stability at high speeds.

GREATER POWER OUTPUT.

Power output on this new model has been increased up to 250 b.h.p. at 6,000 r.p.m. Dry-sump lubrication has been used to cut down overall height and to prevent oil surge and overheating troubles which hampered these cars on tight circuits last year. Disc brakes are again used with an increase in friction lining area and a thickness in the actual disc over last year's type. A small visual indicator is mounted on the brakes to show at each pit stop just how much of the brake friction pads have been used and if a replacement is necessary. The fuel is carried in two flexible tanks which are fitted into light alloy boxes in the tail of the car.

DISC WHEELS.

To reduce weight, perforated disc wheels of light alloy are used with a centre-lock fixing. The cockpit is nicely laid out and is not over-burdened with unnecessary equipment. It contains three instruments —a tachometer, with an inbuilt

Above: With the bonnet wide open the engine and suspension are readily accessible. The oil tank is carried just behind the front wheel.

Below: The famous XK120 engine, this time fitted with three dual-throat Weber carburetters.

speedometer, an oil pressure gauge and a water temperature gauge. The steering wheel is adjustable and is held on its splined column by a screwed clamp. Light alloy spokes and a neat wooden rim are used in true racing tradition. Surrounding the cockpit is a curved plastic windscreen which allows only a minimum of wind blast to reach the driver.

★ SPECIFICATIONS

ENGINE—6 cyl., 83 x 106 mm., 3,442 c.c. Compression ratio, 9 to 1. 250 b.h.p. at 6,000 r.p.m. Maximum torque, 242 lb./ft. at 4,000 r.p.m. Seven-bearing crankshaft. Hemispherical combustion chambers. Overhead valves operated by twin overhead camshafts.

CLUTCH—Three plates, six springs. Hydraulically operated, ball-bearing withdrawal mechanism.

GEARBOX— Ratios: Top, 2.79; third, 3.57; second, 4.58; first, 5.98 to 1. Reverse, 6.1 to 1.

FINAL DRIVE—Hypoid bevel, ratio 2.79 to 1 14:39). Two-pinion differential.

SUSPENSION — Front, independent, wishbone and torsion bars. Rear, trailing link and torsion bar. Suspension rate (at

the wheel) front, 120 lb. per in.; rear, 120 lb. per in.

BRAKES—Dunlop disc. Three-pad front; two-pad rear. Discs: front, 12¾ in. diameter; rear, 12¾ in. diameter. Total lining area: 75 sq. in.; 45 sq. in. front.

STEERING—Rack and pinion. Eight-toothed pinion. 1¾ turns from lock to lock.

WHEELS AND TYRES—Dunlop light alloy, perforated disc, centre-lock wheels.

MAIN DIMENSIONS—Wheelbase, 7 ft. 6 in.; Track (front), 4 ft. 2 in.; (rear) 4 ft.; Overall length, 12 ft. 10 in.; Width, 5 ft. 5-3/8 in.; Height, at scuttle, 2 ft. 8 in.; at fin, 3 ft. 8 in.; Ground clearance, 5½ in. under sump; Frontal area, 10.85 sq. ft.; Turning circle, 32 ft.

I N 1949 a car left the road at the Nurburg Ring and crashed into a grove of fir trees. It was the unlikely start of one of the most successful private motor racing teams since Enzo Ferrari decided to build his own rather than provide glory for Alfa Romeo. The dark blue Jaguars of Ecurie Ecosse would later win outright the world-famous Le Mans Grand Prix d' Endurance in both 1956 and 1957, proving that courage and skillful preparation play a large part in motor racing, even in this heyday of factory teams.

The accident at the Ring happened to David Murray, an Edinburgh businessman and racing enthusiast. His contretemps caused him to consider his responsibilities and especially his wife, who was slightly alarmed at the thought of more tree-felling expeditions. He was thoroughly saturated with the racing atmosphere by this time, and accordingly decided to leave the driver's seat for a managing role. So he formed the Ecurie Ecosse, a racing stable devoted (to the delight of Scots racing fans) to showing just how well Scottish drivers and mechanics could do when given a decent chance. He had a good bit of experience with driving before and after World War II, and knew what to look for in his searches for young talent at Scottish national meetings. All his choices so far have turned out well, but wives and business do take their toll, and the search for new talent still continues.

As a patriotic Briton, he preferred to race British cars, which meant Jaguars (at first C types, latterly D types) in the larger competition sports cars. In the past, Connaught and Cooper-Bristol Formula II cars and smaller sports cars of various marques have raced under the Saltire (the shield of Scotland), but now only the Jaguars are raced in major sports car events. The currently used cars are those of last year's factory team, and one now has a displacement of 3780 cc in view of Briggs Cunningham's success with the bored-out Jag at Sebring. They feature Lucas fuel injection and have the usual D-type monocoque body construction and Dunlop disc brakes. Typically, the Ecurie's cars are painted the dark blue of Scotland's St. Andrew's Cross, and the cars are distinguished by white chevrons painted across the nose to aid pit reconnaissance.

The team can afford to prepare only three cars a year or two old, since financial support on the Mercedes or (even) Ferrari scale is just not available. This means that the cars have to be tuned beyond their previous capabilities. Accordingly, the services of a modern mechanical wizard, W.E. Wilkinson, were bid for and, fortunately, secured. Wilkie looked after the machinery during Murray's own racing bouts, and a successful partnership was happily prolonged when he put power to the dark blue wheels.

Some of the credit for Wilkie's mechanical acumen may be ascribed to his ability as a driver, a rare talent among race mechanics. His training included a stint with George Eyston's Maseratis and some years with the Bellevue Garage, which quite successfully raced a team of MG's at Brooklands (with one W.E. Wilkinson at the wheel on occasion). The traditional view of the oil-covered grease monkey is inaccurate where he is concerned: A salient feature of Merchiston Mews, home of the Ecurie, is that its garages are probably cleaner now than when they were coach houses for the surrounding burghers. Certainly Wilkie and his boys are often to be seen in white coveralls—like doctors conducting a delicate operation in spotless garb.

Mr. Murray's avowed purpose of finding and developing Scots talent has been a resounding success. The first flush of fame came with the two Stewarts, Ian and Jimmy (unrelated), who did very well indeed until the usual family and business reasons forced their retirement from active racing. Currently there are four drivers on call, of whom Ron Flockhart and Ninian Sanderson do the most work outside the United Kingdom. John Lawrence (no relation to the driver who was fatally injured at Riverside) did his share at the Nurburg Ring, Forez and Le Mans, and Desmond Titterington has been active on the Continent occasionally.

Flockhart, a true Scot often seen in the kilt (his is the Ancient Lamont), drives for BRM in Formula I races as well as for Ecurie Ecosse. He is one of the current crop of young British drivers who are well on the way to dominating Grand Prix racing (after Fangio, of course). Flockhart's engineering training stood him in good stead during the testing and development of the BRM and in attesting the excellence of Wilkie's ministrations.

Oddly enough, Ninian Sanderson is a Glasgow man on an Edinburgh team, setting aside an ancient rivalry even fiercer than that between Brooklyn and the Bronx. His experience was in 500-cc Coopers before joining the team, and he has won the Formula III class on almost every circuit in the British Isles, as well as holding a few good hill climb records. A modest Scot, he characteristically gives the credit for a good performance to Wilkie or David Murray, in fact to anyone but N. Sanderson.

There is, of course, a lady behind all this activity; in fact, she's probably at the root of the formation of Ecurie Ecosse. When Le Patron decided to give up racing, one of his major reasons was concern for his wife, Jenny. Once the idea of a Scottish racing stable was broached, however, she became an enthusiastic supporter (so long as husband David did not man a wheel). Since the inception of Ecurie Ecosse, she has been wherever the team goes, lending feminine grace and excellent race recording to a sport largely dominated by men.

This embattled band of Scots does just as its countrymen have done for centuries—a great deal with small resources. David Murray's avowed aim is the world sports car championship, and he may yet pull it off another year. A bad prang in Argentina prevented an appearance at Sebring in 1957. Remember, the next time you hear someone praising Jaguar competition successes, that not all their Le Mans victories are factory victories, and that their sports car championships are also partially due to the giant killers, Ecurie Ecosse, of Edinburgh.

An unusual sort of group, the Ecurie Ecosse Association, may appeal to those impressed by the Ecurie's successes on a shoestring. Its objects are "to support the Ecurie Ecosse motor racing team, to associate itself with the activities of that team, and to do all possible, now and in the future, to maintain successful Scottish participation in motor racing. The badge of the association will be similar to that used by members of the Ecurie Ecosse team.

"It is not in any way a sports car club, but is intended to be on a broad national basis, and it is hoped that branches will be formed wherever the degree of support warrants them . . ."

Further information may be obtained from A. D. M. Dobbie, Interim Secretary, 17, Gordon Terrace, Edinburgh 9, Scotland.—Ed.

ECURIE ECOSSE COMPETITION RECORD, 1957

WORLD SPORTS CAR CHAMPIONSHIP EVENTS

race	length	position
Buenos Aires	1000 kilometers	4th (Sanderson/Mieres), crash in practice
Sebring	12 hours	no entry
Mille Miglia	—	retired at half distance (Flockhart)
Nurburg Ring	1000 kilometers	8th (Fairman/Flockhart), 11th (Bueb/Lawrence), 12th (Sanderson/Steed); team award
Le Mans	24 hours	1st (Flockhart/Bueb), 2nd (Sanderson/Lawrence)
Sweden	6 hours	8th (Scott-Brown/Lawrence)

NON-CHAMPIONSHIP EVENTS

race	length	position
Le Forez	6 hours	1st, 2nd
Monza	500 miles	4th (Fairman), 5th (Lawrence), 6th (Sanderson)
Spa	3 hours	8th (Seidel)

D-type Jaguars: First and second places in the unlimited sports car class at the B.A.R.C.-Daily Telegraph International meeting, Aintree, 1955, were taken by Ninian Sanderson (left) and Desmond Titterington

A Story of Personal Enterprise North of the Border

NOWADAYS, when in almost every sphere of motoring competition cars from this country are meeting foreign opposition on equal terms, a new form of national pride has grown up. The steady upsurge of British products started, so far as sports car racing is concerned, some time ago; recently, it has moved in to Grand Prix racing, the most specialized field of all. Interest in the sport has increased; whereas it received scant publicity before the war, nowadays almost every medium devotes far more time and space to it.

In the sports car field, much of the responsibility for this new-found success has been owed to *Ecurie Ecosse*; it is well, therefore, that we Sassenachs, when we sit back and bask in the reflected glory of Britain's racing successes, should remember that the Scottish contingent has done much to bring them about. The cars are made in England; many of their drivers are English; but it is Scottish enterprise and enthusiasm that created *Ecurie*

Ecosse, and which continues to run it with such success.

When racing was making a somewhat tentative start in the early post-war years, the name of David Murray, of Edinburgh, became well known in the entry lists—usually in connection with a Maserati attached to the Parnell stable. Later, David Murray, and the Maserati, detached themselves from the stable to run independently.

This state of affairs continued happily until, during practice for the 1951 German G.P. at the Nurburgring, the car was involved in a costly and pretty comprehensive accident. The Maserati was virtually a write-off; David Murray escaped practically unscathed—physically, that is. The accident did have its effect on him, however, in that his wife, as so many other wives have done, upped with the rolling pin, as it were, and said "That is enough." David Murray retired from active participation in this type of event.

Unable to race himself, he decided to

do so vicariously, and at the same time fly Scotland's colours on the racing circuits of the world. The idea had been in his mind for some time, and the Maserati's accident accelerated its birth. Thus, in December 1951, was created *Ecurie Ecosse*, a name that has subsequently accumulated more than its expected share of honour and glory.

David Murray was fortunate in already having the services of "Wilkie" Wilkinson—W. E. Wilkinson who, in pre-war years, had been responsible for the preparation and tuning of the M.G. team operated and driven by the Evans family, Kenneth, Denis and Doreen, who ran as a business the Bellevue Garage in southwest London. Since the war, "Wilkie" had been with Reg Parnell, until he left, with the Maserati, to join the David Murray ensemble.

Together they formed the tuning establishment in Edinburgh known as Merchiston Motors, "Wilkie" therefore being responsible from the outset for the preparation and tuning of all the *Ecurie Ecosse* cars.

For the first year of its existence the stable was run on a co-operative basis, the drivers owning their own cars and sharing in the expenses and winnings. The drivers in these early days were Sir James Scott-Douglas, Ian Stewart and W. H. Dobson, and the cars—largely XK120 Jaguars—were immaculately turned out in dark blue. Though sports car racing was their main concern, there was also David Murray's 2-litre, formula 2 Ferrari, which was usually driven by Dobson.

During that season, Ian Stewart took delivery of one of the first C-type Jaguars to be run in private hands, and at once began to score successes with it. Among these were victories in the Jersey road race, and the Wakefield Trophy race in Ireland. The successes scored in this first complete year of active competition are worth recording:

Sir William Lyons presents a bronze Jaguar statuette to David Murray (left), in recognition of the Le Mans achievement. "Wilkie" Wilkinson is on the right

Le Mans, 1956: The only car entered by Ecurie Ecosse takes the chequered flag at the end of the 24-hour race. Inset: Ron Flockhart (at the wheel) and Ninian Sanderson, who drove the car to victory

ECURIE ECOSSE

Date		Meeting		Results
April	6	Charterhall	..	Second.
	12	Castle Combe	..	Second.
	19	Ibsley ..	..	Third.
May	3	Turnberry	..	Two firsts, two seconds, third.
	24	Crimond	..	Second and third.
	29	Isle of Man	..	First in over 3,000 c.c. class.
July	10	Jersey ..	..	First, and first and third in heats.
	27	Charterhall	..	Two firsts and third
Aug.	2	Boreham	..	Third.
	9	Crimond	..	First and second.
	23	Turnberry	..	First and two thirds.
Sept.	6	Wakefield Trophy		First and second.
	27	Goodwood	..	First
Oct.	4	Castle Combe	..	First.
	11	Charterhall	..	First.

If David Murray had been in any doubts as to the wisdom of his plans, this list should have allayed them; it is interesting, incidentally, to note how many circuits in use in those days have ceased to exist. The Castle Combe win late in the season is noteworthy in that Ninian Sanderson, who had joined the team and was Scotland's first formula 3 exponent, was driving a formula 3 car in a formula 2 event!

In the following year, 1953, the team went farther afield, scoring successes at Rheims and the Nurburgring. Many more events were attempted, the cars always being notable for their immaculate appearance and their mechanical reliability, which spoke volumes for the painstaking preparation and tuning by "Wilkie." The list of 1953 successes reads thus:

Date		Meeting		Results
April	12	Charterhall	..	First and second.
	18	Ibsley ..	..	First and third.
	25	Castle Combe	..	First.
May	25	Thruxton	..	First and second.
	30	Snetterton	..	First and third.
June	25	Snetterton	..	Two firsts, second, third.
July	5	Rheims ..	..	Fourth.
	11	Leinster	..	Second and third.
	25	Spa ..	..	Second.
Aug.	3	Thruxton	..	First and third.
	15	Charterhall	..	Second and third.
	30	Nurburgring	..	First in over 2,000 c.c. class.

For 1953, the composition of the team

Surrounded by photographers, and receiving the whole-hearted applause of the crowds, the 1957 winner drives through the pit area

had been altered; Sir James Scott-Douglas remained, and was joined by J. R. (Jimmy) Stewart (no relation of Ian), Ninian Sanderson (who had joined earlier), and J. K. Lawrence, Dickson, P. Whitehead, Curtis and Salvadori also drove the dark blue cars that year. In addition to the three C-type Jaguars, which the team now owned, there were also two formula 2 cars —a Cooper-Bristol and a Connaught. These were run in such events as were available at meetings where the team of Jaguars was already engaged. Perhaps the outstanding of many good performances during that season was Jimmy Stewart's leadership of the British contingent in the British G.P., driving the Cooper-Bristol —until the car crashed only a few laps before the finish.

So satisfactory had the general plan turned out during these first two seasons that the co-operative scheme was abandoned and David Murray became responsible for the whole team. Though he received slight assistance in the capital expenditure involved, the whole financial responsibility of running the team fell on his shoulders; it became essential that it should be run on a self-supporting basis. It had never been intended to make it a money-making concern—there was little hope of that—but the team's original in-

Le Mans, 1957—repeat performance: The two cars entered by Ecurie Ecosse finished first and second. Left: Ron Flockhart (who won), John Lawrence (who finished second), Ivor Bueb (who drove with Flockhart) and "Wilkie," happy after the team's outstanding victory. Right: Ninian Sanderson and John Lawrence, in (and on) the car that finished second

tention to fly Scotland's colours was being carried out magnificently.

At the end of the season the team acquired the three factory C-type Jaguars that had finished first, second and fourth at Le Mans. Until then, the drivers had been handicapped to some extent by driving production C-types with drum brakes against the last word in factory cars from all over Europe. In acquiring these factory "cast-offs," David Murray had equipped his drivers with the best that money could buy—disc brakes and all.

First appearance of the dark blue cars in 1954 was the Buenos Aires 1,000 km sports car race on 24 January. The Ian and James Stewart car, though first away from the start, was soon put out of the race by an accident, but the Scott-Douglas and Sanderson car went through to finish fourth in the general classification and second in its class. This was but the curtain-raiser, and the team continued to score successes at almost every circuit in this country, and many across the Channel, throughout the season.

In the British G.P. meeting, they finished second and third in their class, and at Zandvoort first and third (Sanderson and Scott-Douglas). Roy Salvadori, driving one of the team's cars, won the second sports car race at the September Goodwood . . . by the end of the year the team had competed in 16 events and had been placed in 11 of them.

For 1955, David Murray purchased three D-type Jaguars with which to replace the outclassed, two-seasons-old C-types. The cars were not delivered in time for the Empire Trophy, in which Sanderson finished sixteenth in one of the older cars. At the British G.P. meeting at Aintree he drove one of the D-types for the first time, to finish sixth behind the four victorious Aston Martins and Mike Hawthorn's factory D-type.

The fine drive by Ninian Sanderson and Desmond Titterington in the Goodwood nine-hours' race will be remembered. When the race was nearly over, the Ecurie Ecosse pit staff, whose efficiency as an amateur organization has always been exceedingly good by any standards, stepped up the Jaguar's pace until it began to overhaul the leading Aston Martin, knocking roughly 4sec a lap off Walker's lead. Another 20 laps or so, and perhaps the Jaguar might have pulled it off.

So the success story continued through 1956, with the crowning achievement of all—their outright win at Le Mans. This victory was all the more remarkable for the fact that it was their first attempt at the 24-hour race, and only one car had been entered, as an experiment. To some extent this win was achieved through their adversaries having had trouble—but that is motor racing. This win encouraged Ecurie Ecosse to have another go, in 1957. Two cars were entered for this race—ex-works D-type Jaguars prepared under the guidance of "Wilkie" by his three mechanics, Stan Sproat, Ron Gaudion and Pat Meehan.

One of the cars was fitted with a 3.8-litre engine in place of the normal 3,442 c.c. Jaguar unit, and both cars, as is "Wilkie's" custom, had been taken to pieces, modified in one or two small respects and very carefully reassembled; the 3.8-litre car was fitted with Lucas fuel injection in place of the normal three twin-choke Weber carburettors.

The story of the race is one of clock-work reliability and swift, precise pit work from start to finish—when, as in the previous year, the team scored one hundred per cent success; in 1956, one car was entered—it won; in 1957, two cars were entered—they finished first and second. The winning car, driven by Flockhart and Bueb, assumed leadership of the race after the turmoil of the first refuelling stops had died down—in fact, after a couple of hours' racing.

From that moment onwards the dark blue car led the field, running throughout the 24 hours without mechanical trouble of any sort whatever, and covering 2,732.36 miles during that time. When Tony Brooks' Aston Martin took to the sandbank at Tertre Rouge, and a shunt with Maglioli's Porsche put both cars out of the race soon after 2 a.m. on the Sunday, the Sanderson-Lawrence Jaguar had moved up from fourth into second place, falling in astern of the leading Ecurie Ecosse car. After a little less than two hours the Frère-Rouselle, Belgian-entered Jaguar took second place, only to be held up by ignition trouble at Mulsanne three hours later. This delay let the second Scottish car back into second place, from which it was never again dislodged.

Thus two privately entered Jaguars won the most widely publicized and the longest sports car race in the world . . . a performance which no team, even with the full backing of the works behind it, could hope to better; few manufacturers' teams, indeed, could hope to equal it. The following weekend, at Monza, the dark blue cars were out again—playing a David (Murray)-and-Goliath against the Indianapolis single-seater racing cars in the 500-mile race. Because of the tyre problem, which many considered was extremely dangerous, the Jaguars, with their smaller wheels shrouded—and inadequately cooled—by the mudguards demanded by Appendix C for sports car racing, were limited in speed; at no time were their drivers able fully to extend them.

Yet, despite this imposed restriction, the cars finished fourth, fifth and sixth in the hands of Fairman, Sanderson and Lawrence. In view of the casualty rate among the Americans, and the fact that the intervals between each of the three heats had been entirely occupied in welding-up broken frames and replacing defective dampers, many people felt that, had the race been continuous for 500 miles, the Jaguars would almost certainly have won it.

This performance added greatly to the prestige of the team—if further prestige were necessary after their remarkable Le Mans successes. There is no doubt that their winnings in these two races greatly helped with the team's finances. At a luncheon given in their honour by the Esso Petroleum Company (whose products Ecurie Ecosse uses) during the autumn of 1956, David Murray had said that a crisis had been reached in their affairs. It had arisen, he said, from the needs of the team in the way of capital expenditure—new cars and the replacement of the transporters which, though carefully tended by Sandy Arthur, were worn out. There was a grave possibility that the team would not appear in 1957 events unless the problem could be solved.

Now, to ensure that such a state of affairs does not occur again, and to give Scotsmen the opportunity of contributing to the successes of their national team, an Ecurie Ecosse Association has been formed. It is a very live concern, keeping members up to date with the activities of "Team Scotland," arranging for its members to meet the team's drivers and other racing drivers throughout the world, arranging film shows and talks at various centres in Scotland through the winter months, and providing members with car and lapel badges.

This, and the increasing run of successes of the team, should help keep it financially stable; as the most successful private racing stable of all time, it can reasonably expect full-hearted support from its fellow countrymen.

Next year's plans depend to some extent on the racing plans of the Jaguar company, which withdrew from active participation at the end of last season. Ultimately, the problem of cars is likely to crop up. The cars with which they won this year's Le Mans were a year old; next season they will be two years old, and the Jaguar company has ceased production of D-types. It is almost certain, however, that two dark blue cars will be on the starting line at Le Mans next year, and it is intended that the cars will run in all the races that count towards the Manufacturers' Sports Car Championship . . . but, as David Murray says " . . . with what cars? Aye, that is the question"

Matched against single-seater Indianapolis cars on the banked track at Monza last June, the three Ecurie Ecosse Jaguar sports cars (Fairman, Lawrence and Sanderson) finished fourth, fifth and sixth. Here, Jack Fairman drives high on the banking—anti-clockwise, to suit the American cars

XK "SS"

New Super-performance Jaguar Roadster

Close fitting bumpers—full width at rear and quarter at front—give reasonable protection to the car's purposeful curves. The enclosed spare wheel can be reached without removing luggage or grid. The half-length shielded twin exhaust system hugs the left flank of the body. Right: exceptionally " aerodynamic " in front, the car has only a small air intake and the sidelights are contained in the head lamp fairings

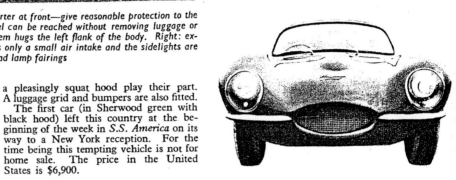

AN exciting new addition to the range of Jaguar sports-racing cars was announced last weekend, the news having already leaked out in America where the first examples are bound. To be known as the XK " SS," it is, perhaps, the most potent two-seater yet to go into production, and it has the full development programme and racing successes of the D-type Jaguar as a background. It is thus closely related to four Le Mans 24-hour race winners.

The power output of its 3½-litre, six-cylinder engine, with three double-choke Weber carburettors, is 250 b.h.p. at 6,000 r.p.m., and the maker's dry weight for the car, fully equipped, is 17½ cwt. According to gear ratios the maximum speed may be up to 170 m.p.h.

Dunlop disc brakes and racing tyres are standard equipment, and for passenger comfort a fully upholstered cockpit, wraparound screen, substantial side-screens and

a pleasingly squat hood play their part. A luggage grid and bumpers are also fitted.

The first car (in Sherwood green with black hood) left this country at the beginning of the week in *S.S. America* on its way to a New York reception. For the time being this tempting vehicle is not for home sale. The price in the United States is $6,900.

SPECIFICATION

Engine.—6 cyl, 83 mm bore × 106 mm stroke (3,442 c.c.). Compression ratio 9 to 1. 250 b.h.p. at 6,000 r.p.m. Maximum b.m.e.p. 175 lb sq in at 4,000 r.p.m. Hemispherical head, twin o.h.c.; three 45 mm dia double-choke Weber carburettors. Lucas coil ignition.

Transmission.—Borg and Beck dry triple plate clutch 7½in dia. Four-speed gear box; synchromesh on upper three ratios (overall ratios, 3.54, 4.52, 5.82 and 7.61 to 1) alternative ratios available; central control.

Final Drive.—Hypoid bevel ratio 3.54 to 1. Alternative ratios available.

Suspension.—Front, independent wishbone and

torsion bar. Rear, trailing links and torsion bar with live axle.

Brakes.—Dunlop disc. Three-pad front; two-pad rear. 12½in dia discs front and rear.

Steering.—Rack and pinion, 16in steering wheel; 1¾ turns from lock to lock.

Wheels and Tyres.—Dunlop light alloy, centre lock wheels. 6.50–16in tyres.

Fuel and Oil Systems.—37 gallons in two flexible tanks. Dry sump lubrication, tank capacity 3½ gallons.

Main Dimensions.—Wheelbase, 7ft 6½in. Track 4ft 2in. Overall length, 14ft. Width, 5ft 5½in. Ground clearance, 5¼in. under sump. Turning circle, 35ft. Dry weight, 1,960 lb (17½ cwt).

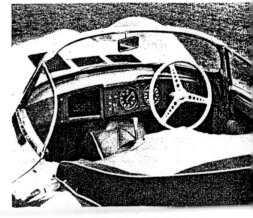

A neat cover encases the hood when it is folded, and a large-diameter, quick release filler cap sits low on the shelf behind the driver. The height of the car is deceptive—it is only 2ft 7½in at the base of the screen. The lines remain most attractive when the hood is raised (below). The simple but adequately equipped cockpit is seen on the right

Jaguar's latest competition car, the XK SS and, behind, a C-type, forerunner of the D-type. Both C- and D-types have been twice victorious at Le Mans

XK SS *Pure Bred and Mettlesome*

WHAT does it feel like to drive a car which is virtually identical with a Le Mans winner? Our Midland Editor supplies that answer in his road impressions of the Jaguar XK SS later in this issue. What manner of machine is this, and how has it come about?

It is a product of a firm who appreciate to the full the value of racing, both to improve their cars and to advertise them to the world. This is the latest version of a car that was designed to win sports car races, and one event in particular. In the XK SS are many standard components common to Jaguar normal series production cars. Consequently there is not the wide gulf separating the production car and the sports-racing car that is to be found in the competition models of some manufacturers. As a result, racing successes gained by Jaguar have a great intrinsic value. The

XK SS is a fully road-equipped version of the D-type competition car, the final stage in the present series of such cars for whose origin we must return to 1949.

In 1948, the XK120 sports two-seater had been introduced, fitted with a 3.4-litre six-cylinder, twin-overhead-camshaft engine destined for the Mark VII saloon. The competition potentialities of this model were quickly recognized by Leslie Johnson, who won the Production Sports Car race at Silverstone in 1949 with one of them, and later persuaded the factory to take an active part in the sport.

The following year saw two private entries of XK120s at Le Mans. At the 20th hour, Johnson and Hadley were holding third place when clutch trouble intervened and the car had to be withdrawn. In September, Jaguar XK120s took the first three places and the team prize in the T.T. at Dundrod.

Meanwhile at Jaguar's the decision had been taken to enter a works team of three cars at Le Mans the following year. An entirely new design was evolved, aimed at raising the power-to-weight ratio, improving the road-holding and reducing drag. To this end, a space-type frame, consisting mainly of steel tubes, was used. Rear suspension was by a live axle, trailing links and transverse torsion bars, and the cars had a lighter front suspension and rack and pinion steering.

The cars were known as C-types, and were enclosed by beautifully proportioned, full-width bodies which have had a notable influence on body designs of Continental sports-racing cars.

That one of the cars won the race at record speed is a matter of history. That they should do so at their first attempt and with a new car was altogether remarkable. The race was not without anxiety for the Jaguar pit staff. Two team cars retired with fractured oil pipes, and it was thought to be only a matter of time before the corresponding pipe failed

Mechanically there is no difference between the XK SS and the D-type. A framed screen and side windows, folding hood, luggage grid and bumpers and the absence of a head rest and tail fin distinguish the car from last year's Le Mans winner

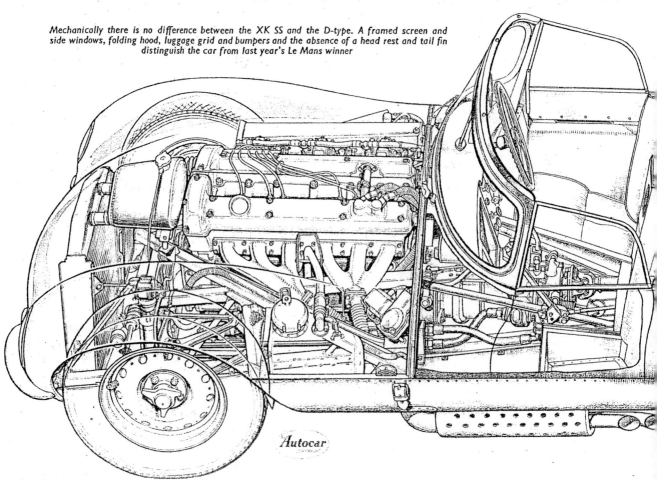

Autocar

on the leading car. Jaguar's racing history hung in the balance on that pipe, for had they lost, they would not have competed again. The pipe held out.

The C-type went into limited production, and was sold only to those who were willing and able to race it. It continued basically unchanged for two more seasons, with progressive increases in power output from the engine.

Le Mans and Jaguar's competition record are closely linked. It is the only European race to receive wide publicity in the United States—Jaguar's chief foreign market. Hence the design of the sports-racing car is determined by the requirements of the Sarthe circuit. For the 1952 race, the bodies were given longer noses and tails. This reduced drag and raised the maximum speed on the Mulsanne straight, but air flow through the radiator was adversely affected, during practice the engines were ruined by overheating, and all cars retired.

There was no mistake about the 1953 race, however. First, second and fourth, record lap and a race average for the first time of over 100 m.p.h. by the winning car, against the strongest Continental opposition, gave an immense impetus to Jaguar prestige. Disc brakes of Dunlop design were used for the first time.

Although the C-type had proved very successful, opposition was expected to be even stronger from Ferrari with their new 4.9-litre model. Also Mercedes-Benz had returned to Grand Prix racing, and were likely to turn their attention to sports car racing, too.

Jaguar's answer was a new competition car, the D-type, embodying revolutionary ideas in chassis construction. It had been found in the C-type that the scuttle, consisting of aluminium alloy panels built to form a box across the car, contributed substantially to the torsional stiffness of the chassis. This principle was extended in the new car by making the entire cockpit section in the shape of an elliptical tube, closed at the front by the engine bulkhead and at the back by a double wall which made use of the curved supports for the seat squabs.

The outer surface of the tube, in which there were openings for driver and passenger, was also the body surface. This was true monocoque construction, and probably the first in a sports car.

A framework of square and round aluminium alloy tubes, argon-arc welded, was tied to the cockpit section around the propeller shaft, and diverged forwards to provide mountings for engine and front suspension assemblies. It was further braced at each side by a square tube which joined the outer extremities of the bulkhead to the centre of the cross member ahead of the engine. The rear suspension was carried on brackets at the rear cockpit wall, and this also supported the containers for the plastic, self-sealing fuel tanks.

Dunlop disc brakes were of a later type, used with a hydraulic servo supplied by a gear box driven pump. The new body shape alone accounted for an extra 17 m.p.h. in maximum speed. When geared for Le Mans, the maximum speed of the C-type was 154 m.p.h. and that of the D-type more than 180 m.p.h. To obtain this, there was a further power yield from the engine which then had dry-sump lubrication.

Wind-tunnel tests with 1/10th size models are used to determine the best body shape, and it was possible to predict maximum speed within 2 or 3 m.p.h.

The 1954 Le Mans race was the most closely fought of all. Although the Gonzales-Trintignant 4.9-litre Ferrari never lost the lead to the Rolt-Hamilton D-type Jaguar, both cars suffered delays in the pits and the issue was in doubt to the end, the smaller-engined Jaguar finishing only one minute behind the Ferrari. Le Mans victories for the D-type in 1955 and 1956 consolidated the model's reputation.

Steel frame tubes were substituted for aluminium alloy on the D-type in 1955. This was done for ease of manufacture and repair, and was found also to give a lighter assembly. The prototype "aluminium" car has, in fact, covered a greater number of racing miles than any other Jaguar, a testimony to the soundness of this all-alloy construction. However, distortion during welding prompted the change to 50-ton steel tubes of 0.020in thickness, and these are Sif-bronze brazed rather than welded, to prevent hardening of the metal around the weld. The tubular frame is now bolted to the cockpit section which remains in aluminium.

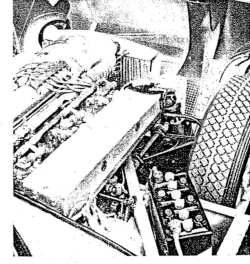

An air duct in the front-hinged bonnet feeds the balance box for the three twin-choke Weber carburettors. Beside the radiator is the oil cooler. Space between front wheel and scuttle houses the battery and brake servo reservoir

This, then, is the background of the Jaguar XK SS, which is the D-type with extra road equipment. Current sports car racing regulations demand a full-width screen and hood. The screen on the XK SS has an aluminium frame, and has been carefully shaped with a generous curve, to reduce drag. The hood folds neatly on to the tail panel, where it is retained in an envelope. It is said to be secure, when erected, at top speed.

Although Jaguar retired from racing at the end of last year, their absence from the sport is only temporary. New low-drag body shapes are being investigated, but mechanically the next competition model is unlikely to be very different from the current cars. With the heartening assurance from Mr. W. M. Heynes, the technical director and the man responsible for the design of the models here reviewed, that they will one day be back at Le Mans, we left the Jaguar works, after a recent visit, with a secure feeling that Britain's prestige in sports cars will continue to be upheld.

Ball-joint suspension, Dunlop disc brake and rack and pinion steering of the XK SS. Holes in the outer flange of the hub receive driving pegs secured to the light alloy disc wheel

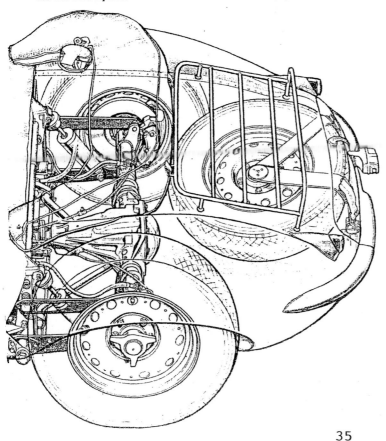

THE XK-SS SOLVES THE TRAFFIC PROBLEM

Speedier cars may be the answer to Britain's overcrowded highways. The faster the car, the sooner it vacates road space for others. With this in mind, Russell Brockbank and J. B. Boothroyd recently took out a Jaguar XK-SS and a flattering amount of short term life insurance

"I see the leaves are on the turn."

RESIDENTS on the test route will not need telling that we followed the line Guildford-Winchester-Salisbury. They will remember us.

There is only one of these motor cars in England, the rest having run off the edge, got stuck under milk tankers, or gone to America, where longer, wider and straighter roads, with fewer tractors towing hay wagons in the middle of them, enable short bursts or maximum speed to be achieved until such time as the police can organize road blocks ahead by short wave. As no more are to be made we had the additional satisfaction of knowing that we were testing the fastest museum piece in existence. The passenger, in particular, found such additional satisfaction welcome. He could do with some. His accommodation was grudging and limited, gouged out of the surrounding mass like a small hole in stiff, hot porridge (the exhaust system travels up his left leg before clotting on the car's left side exterior). His share of the dash cuts him sharply below the kneecaps, or, later, when cringing sets in with the legs well drawn up, across the shinbone. The hand brake will be found to fit conveniently up his right sleeve. The driver, if his shoes aren't too wide, finds no difficulty in depressing the control pedals independently of each other, and can comfortably extend his legs to a squatting position. Over 100 miles per hour he feels the cold, and wonders if there is any quick way of transferring half a dozen hot pipes to his side of the car.

There are four hooter buttons, two of which are sited near the gearshift and tend to be sounded simultaneously with the change—just when, in fact, warning of approach is not needed. It was found wise in our case, when the passenger often wanted to hoot as well, to come to an agreement on whose fingers should fly to which button. This worked well, particularly as the driver tended to use the one in the center of the wheel, which, as it happened, wasn't one.

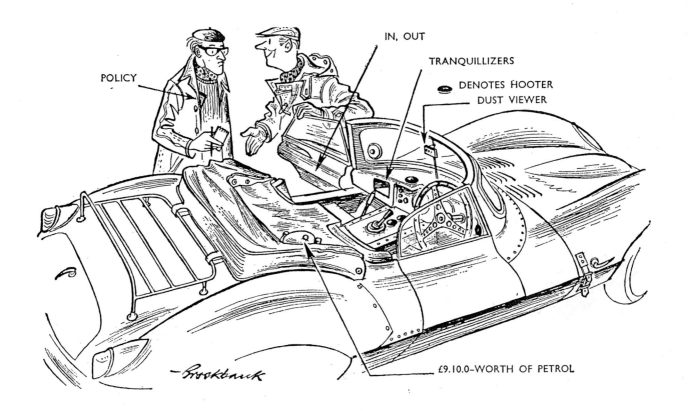

POLICY

IN, OUT

TRANQUILLIZERS

DENOTES HOOTER

DUST VIEWER

—Brockbank

£9.10.0-WORTH OF PETROL

There is no luggage accommodation. Space which might otherwise be handy for trunks, folding perambulators, playpens, sacks of lawn sand and the like is given over to 38 gallons of fuel. The model tested was in British Post Office red, with damp hand prints on the passenger's door.

It was a fine autumn morning with a crispness in the air when, with dry roads and lips, we took off in a south-westerly direction. We at once entered Hampshire, 12 miles distant, at 96 mph, and changed into top. By this time the portion of the passenger projecting above the windshield had the sensation of being embedded in an ice block, though his socks, by way of compensation, were already hot to the touch.

The car was not offensively noisy, so far as it was possible to judge. That is, no adverse criticism was actually heard from scattering road gangs, rocking wayside coffee stalls or a middle-aged couple near Liphook whose picnic was blown up a grass bank. The noise is less a car noise than a pleasing *musique concrete* of wounded bison (engine), nose flutes in ecstasy (tires), and pigs at slaughter (disc brakes); in slow running the orchestration is further added to by spittings on giant flat irons to simulate the six dyspeptic carburetors. This last effect, however, came in only after a rigid throttling down to 70-75 mph to conform to the requirements of built-up area restrictions.

A notable aspect of the test was the good behavior of other motorists noticeable throughout. Even drivers clearly unaccustomed to being overtaken put their curbside wheels on the verge and waved us on just after we had gone past.

Lunch was taken in Salisbury, where some delay was experienced while the passenger, now shaped like an old soup tin pressed for remelting, was pried out by the half-dozen heavy, fresh-faced young men in one-piece caps and fur-collared duffle coats who had been drawn from nearby cars and wished to see, stroke, sniff and otherwise investigate the car. One of these insisted on joining us in the dining room of the Cathedral Hotel, but would neither eat anything nor remove his outer clothing in case we drove away suddenly and robbed him of the spectacle. We tried to turn his conversation from single dry plate clutches and

protected air intakes by asking whether our chosen parking site was police proof, but he dismissed this as meaningless delirium and plunged into some exhaust manifolding on a DB-3-S Aston Martin. He later indulged us by saying that Salisbury was a very pro-motoring city, and never prosecuted cars of over 200 bhp.

On re-entering the car and beginning the return journey it was found that the passenger's lunch was folded up under the breastbone, where it promised to be a lasting obstruction. This proved to have been distributed more equably over the digestive system shortly after Alresford, where a smart piece of braking from 120 mph to a near standstill (58 mph), as a tribute to three busses overtaking two more round a bend, arrested an interesting telescopic lens effect and turned the driver's cap through 360°.

To sum up, the SS isn't everyone's car. Everyone couldn't get in it. It eats up an immense amount of road, converting a 10-mile stretch of straight into something the size of a bus ticket—and thus detracting from the finer points of the scenery. But for the man who wants to leave as much road as empty as possible for other people, who likes to overtake a convoy of six sand-and-gravel trucks with trailers in a space which the ordinary motorist would regard as a tight squeeze for overtaking an elderly lady pushing a bicycle, who doesn't mind having his passenger's shoes on fire and a wife who sits by the telephone with palpitations as soon as the sound of his exhaust has died away, it may be said to exhibit certain points of advantage.

The Lister chassis frame.

Although the 1959 Lister has an entirely new body the gen layout of chassis and mechanical components is unchang except in minor details. Front suspension is by equal len wishbones and Girling co-axial coil spring/damper units; at rear the de Dion assembly is located by twin radius arms an sliding block. Steering is rack and pinion. The 3.8-litre eng illustrated is in unit with a close ratio Jaguar gearbox, and tra mission is taken through a 3-plate Borg and Beck clutch, vi Hardy Spicer propeller shaft, to the chassis-mounted Salisb final drive unit.

The lines of the bodywork and moulded screen/high tail arran ment bear the hallmark of a Frank Costin design. A Cos

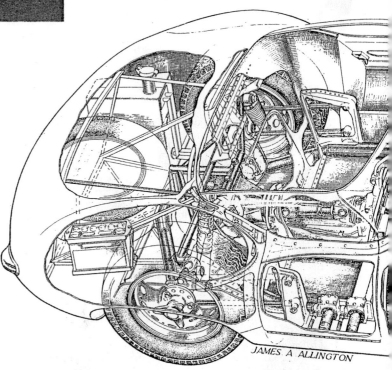

JAMES A. ALLINGTON

Only very rarely are all these people engaged on assembly at any one time, the general rule being three men per car. It is just possible, if the complement in the fitting shop is doubled, to complete assembly in a week, but such rush work only increases the problems which beset George Palmer who, as Production Manager, is responsible for maintaining a steady flow of components and for seeing that every job is finished on—or ahead of —time. George has been with Listers since 1947 and has been concerned with the development of cars from the time when the firm made its first tentative steps into the motoring world.

When the chief chassis and mechanical components have been fitted the car is wired from a loom supplied by Lucas, the various electrical items finally being connected and tested by the Cambridge Battery Service Ltd. Assembly completed, the car goes to Sitton and Mothersole Ltd., another Cambridge firm, for spraying. The works car illustrated is finished in an impressive shade of dark green with a primrose yellow Lister stripe.

Frank Costin's work on airflow is not confined to bodywork and mechanical components, for the driving compartment of the

Front suspension of the 1959 car features modified wishbones and king pins.

new car, which is far more spacious and comfortable than on previous models, is to be fully air-conditioned. Most notable feature of the cockpit at present, however, is the thick padding of the new seats, which have been specially designed by Cox and Co. (Watford) Ltd. And as well as providing increased comfort for both the driver and a passenger, the 1959 Lister has accomodation for a full-size suitcase in the "boot."

As mentioned above, in basic layout the 1959 Lister is unchanged. In addition to the modified wishbones and kingpins the 1959 cars will be fitted with Dunlop disc brakes—as well as Dunlop wheels and tyres—and the Girling suspension units will continue to be modified by Listers to their own specification. The work carried out on these components involves shortening the whole unit, welding on abutments and making up spring retaining washers. For

its early trials the works car used a somewhat makeshift fuel tank but it is hoped to fit fireproof rubber tanks before the start of the season.

The 1959 works cars will be prepared and maintained in a separate premises by a team of racing mechanics led by Dick Barton. Although small, the works "garage" has facilities for welding and crack detecting, so that preparation can be carried on without any interruption of the production programme.

Don Moore, who has his own workshop in Cambridge, will continue to assemble and tune the Jaguar engines fitted in the works cars; 3-litre units will be used for Championship events—plans for the season include the Nurburgring 1000 Kms and Le Mans —and 3.8-litre engines will be fitted for British (and other) unlimited capacity races. It is noteworthy that Listers have found

38

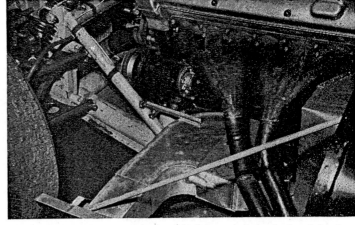

Ducting for the new oil cooler, which has an air intake just behind the nearside front wheel and exhausts into the cockpit.

patented tonneau cover, which is essential to the whole conception, will be added later. The only break in the smooth, aerodynamic profile is a blister on the bonnet which is necessitated by the height of the Jaguar power-unit; it also serves as a convection release for underbonnet air.

Dimensions : Wheelbase, 7 ft 6¾ in; Track—front, 4 ft 4 in—rear, 4 ft 5½ in; Overall length, 14 ft 4¾ in; Overall width, 5 ft 7 in; Overall height, 2 ft 7 in at scuttle, 3 ft 2 in overall; Ground clearance 4¼ in at sump, 6 in at chassis; Turning circle, 40 ft; Dry weight, 15½ cwt. The shape of the fuel tank is not yet finalised, and is not shown in the drawing.

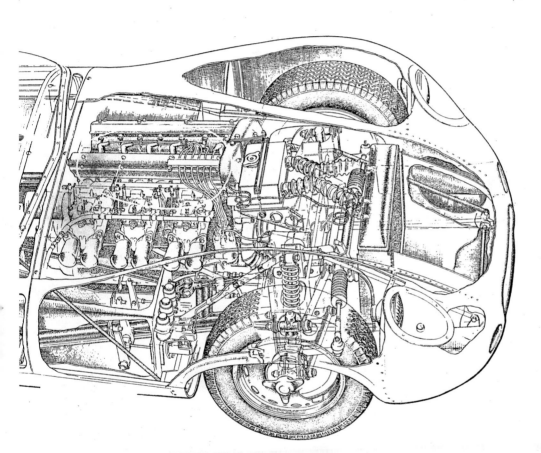

With Frank Costin now employed full-time as Chief Designer, it is reasonable to regard the 1959 Lister as an interim model, to be followed at a later date by an entirely new conception. Despite his association with space frame structures, Costin has a great regard for the twin-tube (or ladder type) frame as employed on the Lister, and considers such a structure vastly safer than an inefficient space frame.

Behind racing—and commercial—success, often given little credit for their efforts, are the men who do the donkeywork. There is a friendly atmosphere at Abbey Road and despite the usual moans and grumbles, one gets the impression that most of the men are happy at their work.

Brian Lister is never slow to give praise for a job well done, and his interest in the men's welfare is shown in the excellent heating system he has installed. In general, he finds, new staff either leave in a few hours or stay for ever. Adaptability is almost as important as a skilled training in any particular sphere, and within a few years the firm has built up a nucleus of employees who can not only "turn a hand" to almost anything, but can do it well. They all show a keen interest in the racing activities of the cars they produce and almost every one of them goes to the circuits at one time or another. They should find their 1959 outings most satisfactory.

Ducting for the rear disc brakes, which is at present made by Williams & Pritchard.

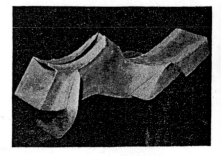

the Jaguar engine by far the cheapest, from the maintenance point of view, that they have ever used; the engine maintenance bill for the much-raced 1957 works car was under £50. Brian Lister finds the personnel of Jaguar Cars Ltd. exceptionally helpful, and he, in his turn, has provided Jaguars with an extremely useful means of testing their engines—particularly the 3-litre unit—while their racing programme was in abeyance. Early last season a certain amount of piston trouble was experienced, but this has now been overcome.

In 1959, in addition to the various proprietary components already mentioned, the works cars will use Lodge plugs and BP fuel and oil.

Apprentices play an important part in the work of the Lister organisation, and the experience they gain in working on the cars, and in travelling to race meetings with the works team is obviously going to stand them in good stead in the future; in this way Listers are also contributing to the ranks of skilled racing mechanics, to whom the development of British motor racing owes a great deal.

The first appearance of the 1959 car will probably be made at Sebring, where one has been entered by Briggs Cunningham.

Magnificent missile

Jerry Ames visits Brian Lister and samples the new
Lister-Jaguar with Archie Scott-Brown at the wheel

THE Lister-Jaguar sprang quickly to fame by winning
the British Empire Trophy early in the season—no
mean achievement for a small concern building
specialist cars against such formidable opposition as works
Aston Martins and other very fast machinery. Since that
outing at Oulton Park the Lister-Jaguar has won other
notable victories—a tribute to the soundness of its design
and the thorough workmanship of Lister Engineering. The
car has always been driven by Archie Scott-Brown, who
has also carried out all the testing, and this combination is
proving virtually unbeatable, at any rate on the tighter of
the home circuits. Indeed, the Lister-Jaguar must be regarded as one of the outstanding sports cars of the year
to date, and has taken circuit records at Oulton Park and
Snetterton, besides winning important races at Goodwood
and Crystal Palace.

Therefore when Brian Lister invited me to his works to
look at the car and sample its roadholding with Archie
Scott-Brown over several laps of Snetterton circuit, I
proceeded to Cambridge with almost indecent haste.

'Come in and have a look round', said Brian. 'We are

not very large, but we do take a pride in our work and
employ good craftsmen.' I soon saw what he meant. Work
can never be lacking in variety at Lister Engineering, a
firm founded by Brian's grandfather in 1890. In its many
departments there are extraordinarily different varieties of
work in progress. In the well-equipped machine shop
men were working on prototypes for industrial purposes.
Next door in the forge others were restoring a superb
example of wrought ironwork, originally made in 1750
by a famous smith. An interesting point: the craftsman
concentrating on re-building an intricate piece of this
delicate tracery was the man who fabricated the special
fuel tanks for the Lister-Jaguar. These men are more than
ordinarily skilled. Now I began to understand why the
Lister-Jaguar consistently puts up such a tremendous performance. There is a painstaking thoroughness for detail
here that is rarely found outside a continental Grand Prix
racing shop. In the corner of the modest works is the
Lister racing department, small, but light and very clean;
and there stood the car stripped of its body, ready for
some new brake temperature tests.

Heavy venting in the back
of the Lister-Jaguar assists
cooling of rear end

Front suspension is by equal wishbones and coil springs enclosing telescopic dampers

First of all I was shown a spare frame of light, yet robust structure. 'Just examine that welding' said Brian. It was as neat as any I have seen. All joints to be welded were first milled to close limits until a good metal to metal fit was obtained, and thus only a minimum of weld material needed. This provides a better joint and prevents distortion.

The main frame members, tapered at both ends, are constructed of three-inch, 14 gauge Class B seamless, solid-drawn, mild steel tubing; the essential cross members being of the same material. To carry the equal length wishbones at the front, steel boxes of 16 gauge steel are used. These are bored on a lathe. A stressed skin, which further stiffens the front end is employed and extends just beyond the oil cooler on the right of the Marston radiator.

The de Dion lay-out at the rear has coil spring-cum-damper unit as at the front

Pop riveting is used to attach the stressed skin to half-inch 20 gauge tubes, shaped to the body profile. Helical springs enclosing Girling dampers are used all round. Those at the front being anchored at the top to lugs on each suspension box and at the bottom to the lower wishbones. The rear springs are attached to struts that form part of the rear unit bracing which carries spring stresses and torque reaction. The differential unit is also located at the top and bottom, additional strength being imparted by a flat horizontal plate bolted up with the differential casing. The hypoid unit is of Salisbury manufacture with a ratio of 3.54 to 1.

The de Dion axle is constructed of three-inch diameter steel tubing, and this design feature is a very important asset to the riding and handling qualities of the Lister-Jaguar. Short, exposed drive shafts, each with two Hardy Spicer joints, convey power to the 16 inch Dunlop perforated disc wheels at the rear.

Girling disc brakes are used all round. The discs having been increased recently in diameter to dissipate heat more effectively round twisting circuits like Oulton Park. Those at the rear are inboard and the pads now work in 10-inch discs, whilst the outboard brakes at the front use 11-inch discs. Recent tests showed the new brakes to be a big improvement on those used in the British Empire Trophy.

As on some other specialist cars, Morris Minor rack and pinion steering with a single universal joint is used. This needs only two turns from lock to lock and provides very light, precise steering. This particular car has an extension piece by the steering wheel, as Archie Scott-Brown prefers a longer steering column than most drivers.

Of course the wonderful six cylinder twin-overhead-camshaft 'D' Type Jaguar engine is a natural power unit to fit into this superb road chassis. It is used in standard form in unit with the Jaguar gearbox and details are well known to most readers. Dimensions are 83 x 106 m.m. giving a swept volume of 3,442 c.c. A compression ratio of 9 to 1 is used which provides 250 b.h.p. nett at 6,000 r.p.m. Maximum revs are 6,200. Fuel is pumped to three double-choke Weber carburettors by two S.U. electric pumps from twin rear tanks, with a total capacity of 20 galls. These are mounted corner-wise in the tail of the Lister-Jaguar. On the exhaust side two clusters of pipes emerge from the engine and are carried to a single silencer with double exit pipes just below the passenger seat.

The attractive streamlined shape of the body, panelled in aluminium alloy, offers low drag properties that are an important aid to top-end performance and yet allow plenty of air to circulate around brakes and tyres. The nosepiece presents a small frontal area and conveys adequate air to the oil and water radiators, carburettors, brakes and cockpit by means of three ducts. Behind the driver a head-rest fairing blends nicely into the streamlining of the tail. On this particular car a single wraparound windscreen deflects air over the driver's head. The pedals are specially positioned for Archie Scott-Brown, which means that anyone of longer stature cannot sit properly in the driving seat, with the result that I was unable to handle the machine. However Brian Lister has kindly promised to have another car available at a later stage, a date I look forward to with keen anticipation!

The Lister-Jaguar is no temperamental racing car that needs to be towed or transported to race meetings, but a practical sports car that can be handled on the road by any competent driver. Scott-Brown drove it the forty miles from Cambridge to Snetterton, and I was interested to note its flexibility even in heavy Newmarket traffic, where horses have pride of place over motor cars.

On arrival at Snetterton I donned a hard hat and visor

—very necessary, for the wrap-round screen protects only the driver.

'I am afraid you are going to have a very uncomfortable ride', said Brian Lister, as I squeezed myself as far down into the cockpit as possible. Surprisingly enough I found more leg room and protection than in a works 'D' type Jaguar. Archie grinned sympathetically as he pressed the starter button, instantly bringing to life the powerful Jaguar engine. As he let in the clutch we moved away smoothly, but at a good rate of knots. Suddenly the acceleration of the Lister-Jaguar became positively staggering, more closely approaching that of a Formula I machine than anything I have ever ridden in yet. Although we were trying larger 7.00 x 16 Dunlop tyres on the rear wheels, 100 m.p.h. was reached from a standstill in 10.5 secs! It was so unbelievable that I made several checks; it was worth it to repeat that fantastic acceleration. Bottom end performance is distinctly good, but once 4,000 r.p.m. had been reached the needle fairly shot up to 5,800 r.p.m. in the gears, nor did it waste any time in top.

Scott-Brown with the author prepare
to test the Lister at Snetterton

It is said that the Jaguar power unit tuned by Don Moore produces no extra power—but the horses must be exceptionally healthy!

Cockpit view showing tilted tachometer and specially positioned Derrington wheel. Even the pedals are drilled!

As Archie normally takes off at 4,000 r.p.m. it was impossible to get a really accurate reading giving the equivalent for 0 to 30 m.p.h., but as near as one could judge the time would be approximately 2 secs. This was in bottom gear of course. In point of fact the lowest ratio produced a maximum speed of 72 m.p.h. The 0 to 70 m.p.h. figure, also obtained in bottom gear took the incredibly short time of only 5.8 secs. All these times were taken with the same slightly larger tyres than fitted for the Empire Trophy. Second gear produced a maximum speed of 93 m.p.h. and third, 120 m.p.h. Archie usually changed into top at 114 m.p.h. The top speed of this car naturally varies according to the gear ratios and tyres fitted, but on this day it was calculated at 154 m.p.h. The maximum I saw recorded was 5,300 r.p.m. in top, which I was afterwards told equalled 138 m.p.h. Believe me, it was pretty draughty at these speeds without a screen and one really had to hang on, but the actual *ride* was never uncomfortable. The steadiness of this machine through the curves was quite a revelation and it is obvious that the de Dion back end and the Lister Chassis and suspension are an enormous help in getting the best from the beautifully smooth Jaguar power unit. There appeared to be no great amount of oversteer or understeer. Fairly neutral steering characteristics have been achieved; but as Archie Scott-Brown likes all the oversteer he can get, he induces this with his throttle foot. Riding with Archie is a pleasure. He is fast, very fast, and none knows better than he how to get the full tremendous performance from the Lister-Jaguar. I can truly say that I never had a moment's qualm. In fact he inspired me with every bit as much confidence as most of the best top-line Formula One conductors I have ridden with.

Brian Lister tells me that he is contemplating producing a small batch of Lister-Jaguars and they will cost the fortunate owners between £2,400 and £2,500. He seems likely to have a queue of competition drivers, cheque-book in hand! It should be about the best value for money today among bigger sports cars ready to race.

SPECIFICATION OF LISTER-JAGUAR

Engine

No. of cylinders and arrangement:	6 cylinders in line
Bore and stroke:	83 × 106 m.m.
Displacement (capacity):	3,442 c.c.
Valve position:	Overhead, with twin camshafts
Compression ration:	9 to 1
Max. b.h.p.	250
at r.p.m.	6,000
Carburettors:	Three twin choke Webers
Fuel pumps:	Two S.U. electric pumps
Tank capacity:	20 gallons
Sump capacity:	Dry sump. Tank 5 gallons
Oil filter:	Tecalemit full flow
Cooling system:	Water pump. Marston radiator
Battery:	12 v. 40 A/H

Transmission

Clutch:	Borg & Beck. 3 plate, 6 springs, hydraulically operated
No. of speeds:	Four
Gear lever position:	Remote control
Syncromesh on:	1st, 2nd, 3rd and top
Overall ratios:	Top: 3·54 to 1
	3rd: 4·525
	2nd: 5·825
	1st: 7·610
Final drive:	Hypoid 3·54 to 1 by Salisbury

Chassis

Construction:	3″ × 14G. Seamless drawn steel tube
Brakes:	Girling disc: 11″ dia. front 10″ dia. rear

Suspension:	F. equal length wishbones and coil springs
	R. de Dion and coil springs
Shock absorbers:	Girling telescopic
Wheels:	Bolt on light alloy
	F—4½ × 16″
	R—5 × 16″
	Dunlop perforated disc
Tyre size:	F. 5·50 × 16 R. 6·50 × 16
Steering:	Rack and pinion
Steering wheel:	Derrington light alloy, leather covered. 15″ dia.

Dimensions

Wheelbase:	7′ 5″
Track:	F. 4′ 2½″. R. 4′ 4″
Overall length:	12′ 11½″
Overall width:	5′ 1″
Overall height:	2′ 5″ at scuttle
Grond clearance:	Sump 4″. Chassis 6″
Turning circle:	32′
Kerb weight:	15½ cwt.

Performance data

Top gear m.p.h. at 1,000 r.p.m.	24	
Weight distribution dry:	F 48 per cent.	
	R. 52 „ „	

3·54 axle ratio   7·00 × 16 tyres

0 to 50	3·8	secs.	1st gear
0 to 60	5·0	„	1st gear
0 to 70	5·8	„	1st gear
0 to 90	8·2	„	2nd gear
0 to 100	10·5	„	3rd gear
0 to 120	13·8	„	3rd gear

Maximum speed in top gear: 154 m.p.h.
Maximum speed with 6·50 × 16 tyres: 145 m.p.h.

AMERICAN VIEWPOINT ON THE
LISTER JAGUAR

by

STEPHEN F. WILDER

and

KARL LUDVIGSEN

*Moss wins the sports car race preceding the 1958
British Grand Prix with the latest Lister-Jagur*

THE latest in a series of sports cars designed more or less expressly for the late lamented Archie Scott-Brown, Brian Lister's 1958 model is definitely at home on both fast and sinuous tracks. It is made in Cambridge, just forty miles down the road from the 2.7 mile Snetterton race course. Here, as at Oulton Park, Archie was absolute king, regularly trampling the opposition under his wheels. He had been doing this for several years, in a procession of Listers powered by a variety of engines.

Skipping the Austin Seven stage on which so many British designers cut their teeth, Brian Lister's first car was powered by the ubiquitous, highly tuned M.G. TC engine, This was in 1954. Before the year was out, he had moved to the 1,991 c.c. Bristol engine, enabling Archie to mow down even the high-priced opposition from the Continent at that Silverstone International meeting. This was the model which put Brian in business of building cars, as well as ornamental ironware, but still unsatisfied, he bought a Maserati engine of the same size in an extravagant attempt to reduce the car's frontal area. (The Bristol, although highly receptive to skilled tuning, is one of the tallest engines around). This car never materialized as the threat it appeared to be on paper, perhaps because even the most skilful tuner requires time to learn his way around a strange engine—and also, perhaps, because with Maser parts as scarce as hen's teeth in England a certain amount of caution may have been exercised.

In 1957 he went native in a big way and came up with a D-type Jaguar-engined *bolidé* that provided Archie with some of the rides of his life. In 14 races entered, he and this first Lister-Jaguar won 11 of them. In every case he equalled or bettered the existing lap record for sports cars.

When, in the latter part of that year, the *F.I.A.* made their controversial announcement that the 1958 Sports Car Championship would be limited to three litres, not everyone could pull an Enzo and dip into a bagful of old bores and strokes. Briggs Cunningham, who had been carrying the Jaguar banner in the United States just as successfully as the

Ecurie Ecosse had in Europe, found himself in a quandary. Even at the beginning of that season, he had had good reason to wonder about his chances with the several-years-old D's. But with the able assistance of Alfred Momo, who had led the way to the 3.8 litre version of the "works D" engine, he was able to enter at least one perfectly prepared car in nearly every SCCA event. And with Walt Hansgen at the wheel, this brilliant car/driver combination out-pointed the more showy but less durable opposition.

But if the engine now had to be *reduced* in order to compete internationally, the D-type just wasn't the car to put it in. At Sebring '57, a 3.0 Maserati easily out-distanced the 3.8 injected D-type. A de-stroked 3.0 could hardly be expected to do better. Reliable to a fault, the D's are simply too heavy for their power to compete any longer.

Cunningham's private experiments, based on the C6R chassis dating back to 1955, had sadly not yielded anything worth following up. This complex Weaver-designed machine destroyed its three-litre "Offy" engine in an Elkhart Lake practice session and lay dormant and dust-covered through 1956. A promising plan to install a "Chevy" V8 fell through, and a Jaguar was finally fitted. It appeared in this form for many 1957 practice runs, but was never raceworthy. A D-type nose section was grafted on, and ducting cut in to ventilate the final drive/inboard brake unit, but compared to a D, the C6R always suffered from poor braking and indefinite steering. This was too bad, because the CR6 has what the D-type needs: some 200 less pounds overall and lighter unsprung members at the back.

Knowing that the Lister-Jaguar's record in English racing was achieved not only by Archie Scott-Brown's remarkable driving, but also by the car's excellent traction, its "stick-ability" at the rear, and not least, by its weight, quoted at several hundred pounds under that of the D's, Briggs Cunningham decided that the Lister might be what he needed to revitalise his flagging racing programme. (At the '57 National at Watkins Glen, Holbert was a too-close second in a 1½ litre Porsche, which at Riverside, Hansgen got it from the other side, finishing fourth to four-plus litre Maseratis and Ferraris.) To Briggs, the Lister looked like the E-type that was required but not forthcoming from the Coventry factory.

In connection with arrangements for the forthcoming America's Cup sailing contest, Briggs visited England in the fall of '57 with Alf Momo and Walt Hansgen in tow. They found Brian Lister's car-building facilities very small but neat, and only part of a substantial iron-working and engineering business. While still adequate, much of the machinery dates back to the 1890's, when Brian's grandfather started the concern.

The 1957 Lister-Jaguar was trailered out to the Snetterton course, and turned loose in the hands of Scott-Brown and Hansgen. Walt liked the car very much—particularly its high cornering speed and the De Dion rear's traction—and posted a time just a second longer than Archie's best for the course.

All parties satisfied, Cunningham placed an order for three cars, two to accommodate a Jaguar engine and the other—at last—to be built around the larger yet lighter Chevrolet V8. The first two showed up at Sebring and the "Chevy" version was expected to arrive in June or July.

The word got around back in the United States and the following jumped to sign themselves up as distributors:

Unusual high tail of car is level with windscreen giving good airflow and at the same time allowing a very large fuel tank to be accommodated. Louvres at base of and rear of body permit dispersal of hot air from brakes and final-drive

Tom Carsten of Tacoma, Washington; Caroll Shelby of Dallas, Texas; and Auto Engineering of Lexington, Mass. They are all more interested in the Chev V8 version, the first of which should be racing by the time you read this. It will be in the hands of Red Byron under the sponsorship of Kelso Autodynamics, and with Red's extensive experience in "pro" racing circuits, it should really get out and move. With all the car orders that have been rolling in, it looks as if Brian Lister (Light Engineering) Ltd., will soon be forced right out of the ornamental ironwork business!

The 1958 Lister is a refined version of the '57 car whose successes have already been mentioned. Changes were based not only on Lister's experience but also on certain suggestions of Alfred Momo. Basically it is still the same as its predecessors, being characterized by a tubular steel frame with unequal wishbones at the front, a De Dion set up at the rear, and coil spring damper units all around. This sounds like a magic formula for successful road racing machinery these days, but it's not as easy as all that to build a champion.

Like most successful specials, the basic car is very simple. Two main side tubes outline the frame, which is widest just under the seats. It tapers sharply inward at the rear and more gradually up to two boxed uprights at the front. These are joined by two cross tubes, and there are two more under the seats.

Main tube diameter on the '57 Lister was the same as in the M.G. and Bristol-powered cars: three inches. Gauge was

Frontal area is little larger than that of many 1,100 c.c. sports cars. Bonnet is bulged to cover the tall Jaguar engine and screen is mounted on scuttle which is a few inches lower than the bonnet "bulge". Outer slots in nose duct air on to the front brakes, while centre mesh grill protects oil cooler and radiator

increased from 16 to 14, however. Designed for more rugged, long-distance use the '58 tubes are four inches across and still 14 gauge. Alf Momo felt that 16 gauge was adequate, and Lister agreed; but mild steel to that specification could not be located in time.

Springing all round is by the popular Girling coil spring/damper system, the concentric units being canted inward roughly 40 deg. at front and rear. Compared to the Bristol cars, the rear coils have been increased in diameter and leaned inward more sharply—both measures to decrease the height of the tail section (increasing coil diameter allowed a reduction in length). Rear springing units are also anchored in a triangulated framework instead of boxed or tubular uprights, as before.

Parallel, equal-length wishbones attached to M.G.A. spindles guide the front wheels. These A-frames are neatly fabricated of tubing, and pivot on bronze bushes at the frame. There is no torsion anti-roll bar, which keeps the two front wheels fully independent. The steering box, mounted ahead of the suspension, is a Morris Minor rack and pinion gear giving but two turns lock to lock.

In 1957, production-type Girling disc brakes were fitted all around, with 11-in. front discs and 10-in. discs inboard at the rear. For long-distance racing, the quick-change pads were needed, but these Girling units were sewed up tight by Aston-Martin. Suitable negotiations by Briggs himself cleared up this difficulty and the 1958 cars have these items, fitted to 12-in. discs front and rear.

For short races, unsprung weight was kept down by attaching the Dunlop light-alloy disc wheels with bolts but this year, for long distance races at least, three eared hub caps will be used.

Rear suspension on the Lister is by a now-classic form of the De Dion pattern. Parallel trailing arms locate each hub fore and aft, while a bronze block on the axle tube slides between vertical guides to give the wheels lateral placing relative to the frame. The 3-in. De Dion tube bends behind the differential and is fabricated of three straight sections, the centre one being but 6 in. long. Welds joining the sections are buttressed by gussets, as are the ends of the radius rods, the wishbones, and other such highly stressed members.

Half shafts are short and simple with Hardy Spicer universal joints and splines. A salisbury final drive unit with hypoid gears and a Dana limited-slip differential ("Positrac-

LISTER JAGUAR

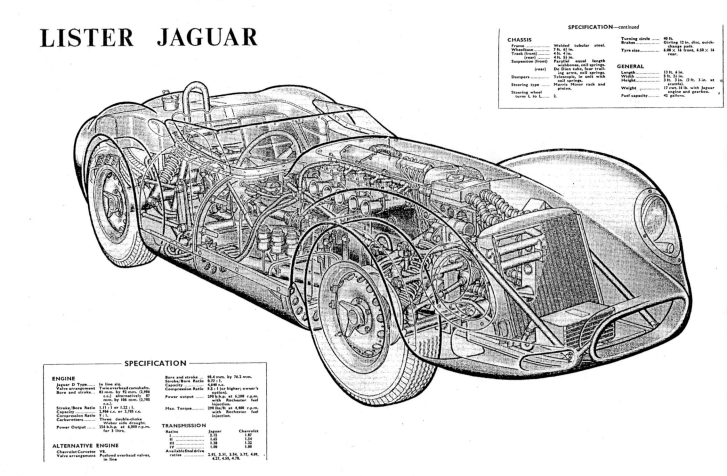

SPECIFICATION—*continued*

CHASSIS

Frame	Welded tubular steel.
Wheelbase	7 ft. 6½ in.
Track (front)	4 ft. 4 in.
(rear)	4 ft. 5½ in.
Suspension (front)	Parallel equal length wishbones, coil springs.
(rear)	De Dion tube, four trailing arms, coil springs.
Dampers	Telescopic, in unit with coil springs.
Steering type	Morris Minor rack and pinion.
Steering wheel turns L to L	2.

Turning circle	40 ft.
Brakes	Girling 12 in. disc, quick-change pads.
Tyre size	6.00 × 16 front, 6.50 × 16 rear.

GENERAL

Length	13 ft. 6 in.
Width	5 ft. 2½ in.
Height	3 ft. 3 in. (2 ft. 3 in. at scuttle).
Weight	17 cwt. 16 lb. with Jaguar engine and gearbox.
Fuel capacity	42 gallons.

SPECIFICATION

ENGINE

Jaguar D Type	In line six.
Valve arrangement	Twin overhead camshafts.
Bore and stroke	83 mm. by 92 mm. (2,986 c.c.) alternatively 87 mm. by 106 mm. (3,785 c.c.).
Stroke/Bore Ratio	1.11 : 1 or 1.22 : 1.
Capacity	2,986 c.c. or 3,785 c.c.
Compression Ratio	9 : 1.
Carburetters	Three double-choke Weber side draught.
Power Output	254 b.h.p. at 6,000 r.p.m. for 3 litre.

ALTERNATIVE ENGINE

Chevrolet Corvette	V8.
Valve arrangement	Pushrod overhead valves, in line.

Bore and stroke	98.4 mm. by 76.2 mm.
Stroke/Bore Ratio	0.77 : 1.
Capacity	4,640 c.c.
Compression Ratio	9.5 : 1 (or higher; owner's option).
Power output	290 b.h.p. at 6,200 r.p.m. with Rochester fuel injection.
Max. Torque	290 lbs/ft at 4,400 r.p.m. with Rochester fuel injection.

TRANSMISSION

Ratios	Jaguar	Chevrolet
I	2.15	1.87
II	1.65	1.54
III	1.28	1.22
IV	1.00	1.00
Available final drive ratios	2.93, 3.31, 3.54, 3.77, 4.09, 4.27, 4.55, 4.78.	

On the car's arrival in the U.S. Briggs Cunningham (right) gave the Listers to Alfred Momo, (left) to check and make any alterations he deemed necessary

tion," etc.) is bolted to the frame. Across its top is a diamond-shaped plate carrying the calipers for the mechanical hand brakes.

The big Lister-Jaguar's tail section has been redesigned to hold a 42-gallon tank of fuel in addition to a six-gallon oil tank for the D-type's dry sump system. This has raised the height of the tail to the level of the windscreen top, reminiscent of the first prototype of the Porsche Spyder. Cunningham's cars has spit-proof rubberized fuel tanks as used on his Jaguars. The windscreen though conforming to the *F.I.A.* rules for height, is a bit of a "cheater" as the tall engine bulge stops just short of the foot of it, enabling its height to be measured from a lower point than one would expect with the fairly tall XK engine. Brian Lister has always been interested in reducing frontal area on his cars; that he has succeeded is indicated by his claim that the 1958 L-J has less frontal area than some current English "1,100s." This may be so, but it should also be pointed out that "some English 1,100s" have much better shapes aerodynami-

cally than the Lister and it's the product of area times drag coefficient that counts.

Throughout the body, the aluminium skin is riveted to a framework of ½-in. 20 gauge tubing which adds stiffness to the whole structure. This is especially the case around the engine compartment and in the nose section, which Williams and Pritchard, Ltd. of Edmonton have managed to make even lower than last year's.

A Marston radiator, with an oil cooler in front of it, is canted steeply back to facilitate the escape of the warm air at the bottom of the car. Two ducts next to the radiator-intake pipe air to the front brake discs.

As mentioned, two of the Cunningham Listers are fitted with the Jaguar engine and the matching D-type gearbox. For S.C.C.A. racing a big 3.8-litre Momo-modified plant is being dropped in, probably with Weber gasworks. At Sebring, though, they had three-litre editions of the famous six.

Calculations based on experience with the engine, and on a conversion by "Wilkie" Wilkinson of *Ecurie Ecosse*, showed that ultimate power output would be higher with a destroked 3.4 block than with the extremely oversquare proportions of a bored-out 2.4 engine. Of course the latter would have required brutal coring changes, too.

At first the Momo Corporation was considered for the task of making up the new crank and rods needed, but Sir William Lyons said that Jaguar would take on the job. Momo and Cunningham are busy enough preparing, entering and racing Jaguar-engined cars in the U.S.A.

The potential output of the 3.0 Jag. engine will probably be 225 to 260 b.h.p. (at Sebring, they were quoted at 265 b.h.p. at 6,000 r.p.m.) If the Listers which Cunningham, received had been as light as expected, namely 1,620 lb. dry (no oil, water or fuel), the cars should have been roughly competitive with the Ferrari and Astons. But they didn't, and they weren't. To everyone's disappointment at the Woodside establishment, the cars tipped the scales at 1,920 lb., putting them back within 50 or 100 lb. of the obsolescent D's. This 300 lb. difference cannot be blamed on the two gauge heavier frame tubing so it looks from here as if the Listers will not figure strongly, if at all, in International three-litre racing. With the well-proven 3.8 engine it will be a different story (as it was in the President's Cup Race), but with the Chevrolet V8, we should see Briggs (and others) pick up where the Corvette SS left off. There's more than a superficial resemblance between these cars, by the way.

In Cunningham's case the engine and transmission unit were supplied directly by Chevrolet, exact duplicates of those used in the SS. Since no further development work has been

Girling disc brakes are inboard at rear close up to the Salisbury differential unit. Canted coil-spring dampers unit are attached to a built-up section of the basic twin-tube frame of 14 gauge ×3 in. steel tubing

Two Marston radiators provide cooling for oil and water and multi-pin plugs carry current for headlamps enabling the body to be completely detached without disturbing wiring

American modifications included mounting the spare with a knock-off cap and moving the battery cradle away from the fuel pipes. Lister's massive fuel tank holds 42 gallons which when full adds much weight to the rear end and provides exceptional traction

carried out on the aluminium heads, the original iron parts were fitted to ensure reliability. The V8 arrived at Lister's shop in October 1957, allowing plenty of time for necessary detail chassis changes to be made. The car's engine room is set well back from the front wheels and is uncluttered, so there should have been no major snags.

At first glance it's legitimate to question the use of a Lister for long-distance racing since it was originally designed for English sprint events. This is partly counteracted by basic changes—the heavy-duty frame, quick-change brakes and knock-off hubs, and larger rubber fuel tanks—and should be fully made up by the detail changes and preparation of Momo in New York.

Cunningham's team plans for this year include the Lister-Jaguars, a Lister-Chevrolet, and the one 3.8-litre injected D-type. One of the remaining D's will retire to the Cunning-ham museum in Connecticut, while the last two will be returned to Coventry, with thanks.

Why the Lister chassis for this new experiment? Those who have driven them say that its most outstanding feature is its road-clutching traction. Full throttle can be applied at any speed in any gear without spinning wheels; excellent usuable acceleration results. The same was the case with the Mercedes 300 SLR chassis, and for the same reasons: 52 per cent of the weight is on the rear wheels when dry, and much more when fully fueled. The Dana differential and low unsprung weight also help out under bumpy and cornering conditions. Torque the "Chevy" engine has, and the Lister should apply it to the road with spectacular results.

This year marked the beginning of an experimental association with Lister, the D-Jaguar acting as a control through the whole programme.

Front suspension is by equal length wishbones with coil-spring damper units. Shackles, and anti-roll bar are fully adjustable. Suspension is "hung" on two perforated boxed uprights joined by two cross tubes

Businesslike-looking cockpit has accessible starter while twin S.U. electric fuel pumps and shut-off valve are situated in the offside door sill. Note windscreen recessed below bonnet bulge

THE 1958 LISTER— JAGUAR

The latest Lister-Jaguar is distinguished by the higher tail; even so, overall height is still only 3 ft. 3 in. Top of windscreen is level with tail, ensuring good airflow

WITH an exceptionally small frontal area for a 3½-litre car, the latest Lister-Jaguar is claimed to offer the best power to frontal area ratio available on a sports car anywhere in the world. Actual area of 11½ sq. ft. (approx.) makes it comparable with many 1,100 c.c. sports/racing machines.

Production of this hand-made car is now well under way at the Cambridge works, and nearly a dozen have been sold, mainly in overseas markets. Most apparent changes from the 1957 models are to be found in the body design. Tail is higher with crashbar incorporated in the headrest fairing and overall height of the body at this point is 3 ft. 3 in. Cockpit layout is well planned and detail finish is of a high standard. A more comprehensive range of instruments is fitted and both seats are fully upholstered. Doors have map pockets.

A larger (38-gallon) fuel tank is fitted and positioned at a higher level and further forward than in last year's car. Twin S.U. electric fuel pumps are located in the door sills where they are readily accessible for any possible fuel feed trouble. The spare wheel rests in a cradle to the rear and partly underneath the tank instead of on top, and an eight-gallon oil tank for the dry sump lubrication system is carried on the nearside adjacent to the spare wheel.

Improved braking is another feature of the new car—Girling 12 in. disc brakes are fitted both front and rear instead of the 10 in. rear and 11 in. front of previous cars.

It is interesting to note that in addition to the 3½-litre "D" type Jaguar engine, a special 3-litre version is to be available which will probably develop power in excess of the standard 3½-litre (210 b.h.p.) engine. Reduction in capacity is obtained by the use of a special short-throw crankshaft of 92 mm. stroke. The standard 3½-litre Jaguar bore of 83 mm. is retained which means that the new engine will gain the twin advantages of higher revs. and lower piston speed. Torque will undoubtedly be slightly reduced but it is unlikely that circuit speeds will be much slower with the new engine.

It is obvious that *Ecurie Ecosse*, *Ecurie Belge* and other

Frontal area is down to 11½ sq. ft., the extremely low windscreen height is attained by dropping the scuttle line below that of the bonnet

formidable teams and drivers will be using this interesting "new" power unit for Lister and Jaguar cars in 1958 Sports Car Championship races. Chevrolet V8-engined Listers will also be available for the American market.

SPECIFICATION OF LISTER-JAGUAR

Engine
No. of cylinders: six in line. *Bore and stroke:* 83 × 106 mm. *Capacity:* 3,442 c.c. *Valve arrangement:* twin o.h.c. *Compression ratio:* 9 : 1. *Power output:* 250 b.h.p. at 6,000 r.p.m. *Carburetters:* three twin choke Webers. *Fuel pumps:* two S.U. electric. *Sump capacity:* dry sump. *Tank:* 5 gallons. *Oil filter:* Tecalemit full flow. *Cooling system:* water pump. Marston Excelsior radiator. *Battery:* 12-volt, 40 amp/hour.

Also available with 3-litre (83 × 92 mm.) Jaguar dry sump engine.

Transmission
Clutch: Borg and Beck, 3-plate, 6 springs hydraulically operated. *No. of speeds:* four. *Gear lever position:* remote control Synchromesh on 1st, 2nd, 3rd and top. *Overall ratios:* Top 3.54 : 1, 3rd 4.525, 2nd 5.825, 1st 7.610. *Final drive:* Hypoid 3.54 : 1. *Optional ratios:* 2.93 : 1, 3.31, 3.54, 3.77, 4.09, 4.27, 4.55 and 4.78.

Chassis
Construction: 3 in. × 14 gauge seamless drawn steel tube. *Brakes:* Girling disc 12 in. diameter front and rear. *Suspension:* front, equal length wishbones and coil springs; rear, de Dion and coil springs. *Shock absorbers:* Girling telescopic. *Wheels:* Dunlop perforated knock-on disc 5 in. × 16 in. *Tyre size:* front 6.00 × 16; rear, 6.50 × 16. *Steering:* rack and pinion. *Steering wheel:* Derrington 15 in. light alloy. *No. of turns* (lock to lock): 2.

Dimensions
Wheelbase: 7 ft. 6¾ in. *Track:* front, 4 ft. 4 in.; rear, 4 ft. 5½ in. *Overall length:* 13 ft. 6 in. *Overall height:* 2 ft. 3 in. at scuttle, 3 ft. 3 in. at headrest. *Ground clearance:* 4½ in. *Turning circle:* 40 ft. *Dry weight:* 15½ cwt. *Tank capacity:* 38 gallons.

Performance Data
Top gear m.p.h. at 1,000 r.p.m.: 24. *Weight distribution, dry:* front 48 per cent; rear 52 per cent.

With fuel pumps located in the door sills access is easy. The cockpit is now fully trimmed and even has map pockets in the doors

1958 LISTER JAGUAR

THE Lister Jaguar, which has already established itself as one of the world's fastest and most exciting sports machines, will appear on racing circuits in 1958 as a sleek and most attractive car. It has an entirely new body, enormous (12 inch) disc brakes, and (for Sports Car Manufacturers' Championship events) a 3-litre version of the Jaguar engine. It is also possible to fit the 3.4 and 3.8-litre Jaguar engines, and the powerful 4.5-litre Chevrolet unit.

The basis of the 1958 Lister is similar to that of the "works" car, with which Archie Scott Brown won eleven races last year, and which has just returned from a winter season in New Zealand. Largely as a result of last year's successes, several orders have been placed for the new model, notably by Ecurie Ecosse, Briggs Cunningham (2), Ecurie Nationale Belge and Peter Whitehead. Five orders have been received for Chevrolet-engined cars, two of which will go to Carroll Shelby, and there is a likelihood that production of one chassis a week will be maintained for some time.

The car illustrated here belongs to Briggs Cunningham and is now in America; it will be driven at Sebring by Archie Scott Brown and American Walt Hansgen who, last October, took the "works" car round the Snetterton circuit in 1 minute 46 seconds.

Most noteworthy feature of the 1958 Lister is the extremely low frontal area. Air-intake orifices are reduced to a minimum, headlamps are faired into the wings, and the overall height at the top of the full width (Appendix C) windscreen is only 2 ft 9 in. The high tail is aligned with the top of the windscreen and accommodates a larger (38 gallon) fuel tank, together with a 5 gallon oil tank.

The view from the driving seat is essentially distant—which it should be anyway, in such a high-performance vehicle — because the top of the engine-cover is almost level with the top of the windscreen. On the (English) road it is unusual to get out of second gear, but even so 6000 rpm in this ratio represents quite a fair speed!

To cope with its potential maximum speed the 1958 Lister is fitted with Girling disc brakes, having

Driving compartment is fully upholstered. Interesting detail is small slot behind doors which provides cooling air for rear brakes.

Brian Lister emphasises the low seating position of his 1958 car. Note steeply-raked windscreen.

12 inch diameter light alloy discs all round. An interesting detail point is the positioning of small cooling ducts for the rear brakes, which are mounted inboard.

Other detail modifications include the use of a cast elektron case for the final drive unit. A range of eight different final drive ratios is available. The spare wheel and battery are fitted in separate compartments beneath the fuel tank.

As has already been mentioned, Jaguar have developed a 3-litre version of their famous six cylinder engine to comply with the Sports Car Manufacturers' Championship regulations. The most notable feature of this unit is that it produces more power (254 hp at 6300 rpm) than the standard 3442 cc D-type engine. The reduction of cubic capacity was achieved by shortening of the stroke from 106 to 92 mm. Bore is unchanged at 83 mm, giving a capacity of 2986 cc. The latest 35/40 degree cylinder head is the source of the increased power output and with a final drive ratio of 2.93 to 1 the Lister should have a maximum speed of over 180 mph.

For races in the "unlimited" category the Lister chassis will be fitted with the 3.8-litre Jaguar, or 4.5-litre Chevrolet engine, from each of which some 300 hp can be extracted. With its very low frontal area, and dry weight of 15½ cwt, the Lister should, in these forms, be capable of over 200 mph. Such velocities can only be *imagined* by the majority of readers, and the number of drivers capable of handling a car at these speeds is obviously limited.

As a "production" model the 1958 Lister is rather better appointed in the driving compartment

With bodywork removed the machinery gives an impression of massive power   *Note oil radiator and sockets for light connections.*

This view of the rear suspension shows twin radius arms, de Dion tube and coil spring/damper unit. Disc brakes are mounted inboard, alongside the Salisbury final drive unit.

Front suspension is conventional by double wishbones, the lower link acting on coil spring/damper unit. Anti-roll bar is also visible, together with large brake disc.

than the 1957 " works " car. Two fully upholstered seats are provided, together with a padded cover over the transmission tunnel. There are shallow pockets in the doors, but the small space to the driver's right is occupied by twin SU electric fuel pumps. Leg-room on the passenger side appears to be rather limited.

The full range of instruments includes a speedometer calibrated up to 190 mph (to the delight of small boys) and provision is made for instrument-lighting. The starter is operated by turning the ignition key.

Two "works" Listers will be raced this year, in addition to the " private-owners " cars mentioned above. Archie Scott Brown's team-mate has not yet been signed-on, and Archie himself will drive an Ecurie Ecosse Lister in selected Championship events. One thing is certain; inexperienced drivers need not apply.

On the eve of a new racing season the prospects for Brian Lister (Light Engineering) Ltd. are decidedly bright. If sports/racing car production can be maintained at the present level it may not be long before the firm launches into the manufacture of a road car. Endowed with the basic characteristics of the Lister-Jaguar, in perhaps slightly less " hairy " form, this could well be an enthusiast's dream come true.

SPECIFICATION
CHASSIS
Construction—3 in., 14 gauge seamless drawn steel tube. Suspension—Front equal length wishbones and coil springs. Rear, de Dion and coil springs. Shock Absorbers—telescopic. Girling manufacture. Brakes—Girling disc, 12 in diameter front 12 in diameter rear. Wheels—knock-on light alloy 5 in by 16 in. Perforated disc. Dunlop mannufacture. Tyre size—front, 6.00 by 16., rear, 6.50 by 16. Steering—rack and pinion. Steering wheel—light

alloy, leather covered. Derrington manufacture, 15 in diameter. No. of turns (lock to lock)—two

DIMENSIONS
Wheelbase— 7 ft 6¾ in. Track—front, 4 ft 4 in, rear, 4 ft 5¼ in. Overall length—13 ft 6 in. Overall width—5 ft 2½ in. Overall height—2 ft 3 in at scuttle, 3 ft 3 in at head rest. Ground clearance—sump 4 in, chassis 4½ in. Turning circle—40 ft. Dry weight—15½ cwt Weight distribution dry—front 48 per cent., rear 52 per cent. Tank capacity—38 imperial gallons.

ENGINE
3½-litre Jaguar engine. No. of cylinders—6 in line. Bore and stroke—83 by 106 mm. Capacity—3442 cc. valve position—overhead, with overhead camshaft. Compression ratio—9 to 1. Maximum hp—250 at 6000 rpm. Carburetters—three twin choke Webers. Fuel pumps—2 SU electric pumps. Sump capacity—dry sump. Tank 5 gallons. Oil filter—Tecalemit full flow. Cooling system—water pump. Marston Excelsior radiator. Battery — 12 volt, 40 amp/hr.

A 3-litre Jaguar engine is also available : Bore 83 mm; stroke 92 mm; 2986 cc. Fitted with the latest 35/40 degree cylinder head and three Weber 45 mm DCO 3 carburetters, this unit develops 254 hp at 6300 rpm.

TRANSMISSION
Clutch—Borg & Beck, 3 plate, 6 springs hydraulically operated. No. of speeds—four forward and reverse. Gear lever position—remote control conventional. Syncromesh on—1st, 2nd, 3rd and top. Overall ratios—top, 3.54 to 1; 3rd, 4.525; 2nd, 5.825; 1st, 7.610. *Final drive—hypoid, Salisbury manufacture. Available ratios:—2.93:1, 3.31:1, 3.54:1, 3.77:1, 4.09:1, 4.27:1, 4.55:1, 4.78:1.

* Incorporates the Powr-Lok differential unit at no extra charge. ZF limited slip differential available at extra cost.

Let loose with the Lister

Functional rather than fashionable, the Lister-Jaguar has all the essentials to suit driver and regulations. Note the wiper and horn

Off the Track, and in the Traffic with Horses to Spare—in the Fastest British Sports Car

SPECTATORS at motor race meetings need feel no shame if sometimes they have difficulty in deciding whether a car is a racing or sports one; the dividing line has worn very thin in places and in many categories performances are equally close.

Appendix C of the International Sporting Code (there are non-appendix C sports car events, too), lays down officially what a sports car must not be without, and how it shall be put together—"coachwork must be completely finished and offer no makeshift element"—hm . . . "floorboards, tubes and castings must . . . be properly jointed together and firmly fixed "—ah. . . .

It then goes on about mudguards, hoods (that need not be fitted during the race), wipers, starter, horn. Cars must have a rear-view mirror (not less than 50 sq cm) and an *efficient* silencer and "the exhaust must not be allowed to raise any dust." And, of course, there is the unused spare wheel—it must not be carried in the cockpit.

Regulations and rules of this sort are often regarded as a challenge rather than a guide. Most of us have suppressed a smile at individual interpretations, particularly at Le Mans. One tends to take the attitude "Good luck if you can get away with it," but it is bad luck on firms like Jaguar and Aston Martin, who usually produce a nicely finished and trimmed car that you would be pleased to take your wife in, both wearing Sunday best.

Now take Brian Lister's sports—RACING car, built for and around Archie Scott Brown. It has been outstandingly successful this season, winning major events at almost every home circuit, against the toughest competition. Some notes on its performance are listed at the end of this story, together with a brief specification. It is at least part sports car and, as such, should be roadable and capable also of carrying two people. Is it, we wondered? Apparently no one had thought much about this, and attention has been concentrated on racing.

Brian Lister agreed that the matter should be put to the test, provided that the car remained intact, was delivered for

Archie at speed: Crystal Palace, 10 June

a day to Venner's factory on the Kingston By-pass, and returned by the weekend to Cambridge. There is always something to learn from such a car that applies to everyday driving, and points the way to future experiences. Herein lies the value.

Clearly young enthusiasts might be biased as drivers for such a test, and as the Chairman and directors were understood to be busy with the Motor Show, the Editor was practically forced to volunteer before anyone else had a chance.

A bright day and dry roads assured an interesting journey from Cambridge. But first, naturally, we looked round the venerable Lister premises, where Brian's father before him dealt in skills and precision with metals.

The Archie car changed in detail in July, chiefly to conform with Appendix C. The head fairing has gone, the screen is full width, head lights, with built-in side lights, are faired into the body just ahead of the wheels, and a 3.8 works Jaguar engine is installed together with some detail equipment.

We asked about driving and handling, but Brian Lister rocked us a little by saying firmly that he had never driven his car. He added that it was no trouble,

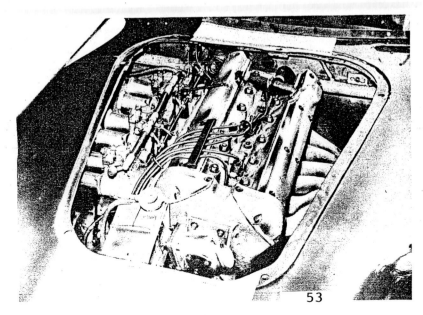

A beautiful 3.8-litre engine, neatly installed and spotlessly clean. It pulls evenly and hard at low r.p.m. and produces 300 real b.h.p.; 100 octane fuel is preferred at 10 to 1 compression ratio

Eager but docile; few cars on the road could be safer at 100 m.p.h., and none passes the figure more easily or quickly. In this prototype the passenger has restricted legroom, and comforts and protection are marginal

and that the clutch had normal road feel. Warnings concerned the two filler caps at the rear, that on the left being for oil, not more petrol; and the restrained use of accelerator when starting from cold. There is no choke.

The engine bay is very full indeed and spotlessly clean. It stayed immaculate for the three days we had the car; we could have eaten breakfast off the cylinder head on the last morning. The big engine, prepared for dual ignition but with six plug holes blanked off, is plain but most impressive with three twin-choke Webers to set it off—and how simple the throttle linkage. Power is only a fraction short of 300 b.h.p. at 5,600 r.p.m. We were given this figure as a normal limit.

The Jaguar engine picture (for Lister customers) is for the moment a little involved. The car at present has a works 3,781 c.c. unit with 10 to 1 compression ratio. A similar engine with 9.25 to 1 compression in Hamilton's Le Man's D-type this year produced 295 b.h.p. maximum (and this car was timed at 178.9 m.p.h. on the Mulsanne straight).

The coming year's international formula specifies a 3-litre limit. Ecurie Ecosse have a 3-litre unit, prepared two years ago. A 3.4 with shorter stroke to bring its capacity down to 3 litres sounds attractive —more so than a long-stroke 2.4. Jaguars are noncommittal at present, but are thought to be co-operative.

And now to the cockpit. Frankly conditions are pretty rugged in this prototype, and sizes and reaches are arranged for Archie Brown alone. But with a car of this kind, which is now to be built in limited numbers to order, you get what you order. Appearance is purposeful and functional rather than beautiful; the new cars will be much more attractive in detail and balance. And the inside will be designed as a whole and well finished, rather than being built in stages and hacked about in the course of development. Appearance and finish will be important

Next year's "production" cars will be similar but sleeker as on the right, and well trimmed and fitted inside

if American orders are to follow that of Ecurie Ecosse.

It is likely, too, that a fair degree of roadability in the sense of comfort and equipment will be appreciated in the United States. A little cow leather for trim, perhaps, even if no tree wood.

It is not an easy matter to get into the Lister-Jaguar, and some leg threading and sliding down is needed. The instruments can be seen in the photograph. The gear lever is short, but feels an inch or so too high for comfort. The rev counter is inverted to make it easier to read the "operative" bit between 3,500 and 5,800 r.p.m.—but that is not to suggest any lack of punch below 3,500. The switches control ignition, two fuel pumps, and lights. The bulb horn is almost inaudible but legal; the road fund licence might be worn on the driver's lapel.

The car started at once and from sound and feel was raring to go. We wondered as we pulled away whether the Cambridge police are proud of their successful local sports car and turn a deaf ear on its approach. We hoped we wouldn't see any police gentlemen but there, at the first roundabout 200 yards from the Lister works, were five of them with a car and two bikes, and there was a lorry stationary across the road to hold us up.

Too much idling might lose plugs; the battery is too small for many starts. Perhaps a winning smile from the driver might help. The nearest officer looked at the side outlet exhausts, pursed his lips

but grinned as we moved off. Later we became less conscious of the straight-through exhaust, but the idling with engine hot became faster and less even.

Soon Cambridge was behind us and we were on course for a disused airfield where we do some of our performance testing. This took us past Archie's garage, but time was now short if the car was to be back in London by early afternoon. Reluctantly we swep' by, not without Archie hearing familiar noises and seeing the tail disappearing to the north-west.

Just a reminder that you are now hearing from an ordinary motorist, not a racing driver; the comments on handling might be your own. The Lister-Jag is truly a very easy car to drive on the open road. The clutch, we have already noted, is gentle, the steering very light and positive and the gear change quick and slick, with synchromesh for all the close ratios in the D-type Jaguar box.

Acceleration at this early stage is faintly alarming, so that one changes up early and takes it in short bursts. An indecisive left hand flicks between steering wheel and gear lever, seldom being on the right one at the right time. Soon, with growing confidence and better anticipation, this sorts itself out.

Even so, the time spent accelerating in any one gear is no more than a few seconds. You can go from 50 to 70 m.p.h. in second gear in 2 sec and these are the speeds at which you might change out of bottom and then up to third if you

were hurrying. May as well leave your hand on the lever.

There is nothing hard about the ride except on poor road surfaces and the engine is beautifully smooth and responsive. Idling, particularly when hot, is distinctly lumpy, of course. We have seldom experienced a flatter ride on corners; this car is a "square" with no idea of rock and roll at all.

If you drive fast you want to know that

In the Lister-Jaguar corners and bends can be taken comfortably at twice the normal speeds and roundabouts, like that shown above, are a pleasure to negotiate

you can stop. The Lister-Jaguar weighs only a little over 15 cwt on the road, and its four discs haul it to a standstill very quickly indeed. There is no roughness or pull to either side, so they can be used very hard with confidence. Until you have warmed them and proved them for yourself, they give an impression of being less good than they are—and the pedal pressure feels quite heavy to produce quick results. This is, no doubt, due in part to the higher than normal speeds at which the brakes are applied.

As this is probably the fastest car on British roads just now, it is not surprising that we have never before experienced such acceleration. Standstill to 100 m.p.h. in 10-and-odd seconds is breathtaking. Rover's JET 1 gave (still gives) the same order of sustained push in the back.

The drive south to London down A1 was most exhilarating. We have never covered it more rapidly nor felt safer doing it. With such acceleration, overtaking the tight-packed streams of lorries becomes as easy as the passing of a single one in an ordinary car. The Lister has adhesion on the sweeping bends to look after higher speeds than we know how to use. Steering is light and precise.

Comfortable cruising speed calculated from r.p.m. was in the region of 90 m.p.h., with frequent bursts up to the 120s. We found that the limit was set by the distance one could see and anticipate the movements of other traffic. We preferred to cut early and brake lightly rather than the reverse. Many times we waited to pass when, in fact, we could have been through with a quarter of a mile to spare; it takes time to judge such acceleration and speed. As it was, we never had a tight moment, and there were always ample reserves of time, space and control.

Fuel consumption depends on how you drive; with us it averaged 14-15 m.p.g.

Looking back, we think the traction must have been outstanding on the dry roads, because with the full urge and acceleration through the gears the wheels spun only with reluctance. There was little tendency, even on wet roads, to indulge in unstable swish-tailing although the back is certainly lively in the rain.

At first one might think to blame the steering for change of feel according to circumstances, but clearly this is a matter of the amount of power through the back wheels. Once the technique is learned, the steering proves on corners to be the willing slave of engine power. Show the nose the direction you want to take and then, in reason, put your foot down. The car will be round the bend and on its way in a moment. If you lift your foot on a fast curve then the car thinks you have changed your mind and prepares to go straight on. The ready response to controls and driver's mood may be likened to that of a well-schooled, oat-full horse.

Not unnaturally, the car was a little embarrassing in London. It has a good 8 to 1 bottom gear and is docile to handle, but the exhaust is too rorty for built-up areas. After long delays through Euston and the Gray's Inn Road, number one plug reluctantly went out. There was many a smile or wave of recognition (of the car)—surprising how well it is known. One old lady in Camden Town told us we ought to be run in. Even so, with only minor changes of pipes and plugs we would happily use the car in big cities.

That night we drove south. Lights and

visibility were adequate for quite high speeds, but when you are sitting about six inches off the ground your eye level is below dipped head light beams and you get well dazzled. Additionally the Perspex screen is a trifle opaque after weeks of racing, and the cold air over the top (sans goggles) was more eye-watering than by day.

The pictures you see were taken early next morning in the Box Hill area when we went out again for the sheer joy of dashing up and down the traffic-free by-pass. We made no attempt at dead accurate timing—the car has demonstrated its abilities in skilled hands on many tracks—again speeds are a matter of skill, gearing, wheel size and road-space. From the Burford Bridge roundabout we calculate we reached 128 m.p.h. (5,600 r.p.m. in top) in 600 yards. The standing ¼-mile figure and speed in present form should be 13sec and 110 m.p.h. The sweeping S bends that follow are right for 90-100 m.p.h. with some power on (Lance Macklin once took us through at 108 m.p.h. indicated on his Facel Vega, but both car and driver are rather exceptional). We assume Archie would take the corner "flat" in the Lister.

Anyone who has seen Archie whip out of the chicane at Goodwood must have wished to be able to do it as neatly. Starting gingerly, we tried leaving a roundabout each time with more speed and power until we had a nice controlled slide to correct. It all adds to experience and teaches you something new about feel and control, and the Lister joins in the fun.

Well that was it; our questions were answered; the party was over. The car is pleasant and easy to drive on the road. It does carry two people, rather uncomfortably if they are bigger than small, but a suit to fit someone else is likely to restrict your movements if you squeeze into it. Our Lister-Jaguar would be bespoke. Brian Lister says that it would cost £2,750 basic or, without engine (so you could fit, say, a Chrysler Fire Power), £1,750.　　　　　M. A. S.

Lister-Jaguar Performances on British Circuits (Driver: Archie S. Brown).

Oulton Park (British Empire Trophy 6.4.57), equalled Musy's sports car lap record in 3-litre Maserati, 1 min 56 sec=85.69 m.p.h.

Silverstone (Daily Express B.R.D.C. meeting 14.9.57) equalled sports car lap record held by Hawthorn in D-type Jaguar, 1 min 47 sec=98.48 m.p.h. Circuit lap record held by Behra in B.R.M., 1 min 42 sec=103.31 m.p.h.

Aintree (20.7.57) In sports car race, 2 min 11.8 sec=81.94 m.p.h., on a wet track. Broke sports car lap record in practice of 2 min 06 sec =85.71 m.p.h. (unofficial). Circuit lap record held by Moss in Vanwall, 1 min 59.2 sec=90.6 m.p.h.

Goodwood (Easter Meeting 22.4.57) Fastest lap, sports car record 1 min 34.6 sec=91.33 m.p.h. Circuit lap record held by Brooks, Vanwall, 1 min 29.6 sec=96.43 m.p.h.

Snetterton (Vanwall Trophy Race Meeting 28.7.57) lowered sports car lap record to 1 min 45.4 sec=92.22 m.p.h. (Salvadori, Aston Martin, also equalled sports car record at Silverstone and holds sports car record at Aintree.)

During the 1957 season the car was entered for fourteen races and won eleven of them. It finished second in another but suffered minor mechanical trouble in the remaining two while in the lead and having already set up the fastest lap in both races.

Brian Lister (Light Engineering), Ltd., Abbey Road, Cambridge.

SPECIFICATION

ENGINE: No. of cylinders, 6 in line; Bore and stroke, 87 x 106 mm (3.42 x 4.17in). Displacement, 3,781 c.c. (230 cu in); Valve position, twin o.h.c., hemispherical head; Compression ratio, 10 to 1; Max b.h.p., 300; Carburettors, three twin-choke Weber. Fuel pump, two S.U. electric. Fuel tank capacity, 35 Imp gal. Oil, dry sump, tank capacity, 5 Imp gal; Oil filter, Tecalemit full-flow; Cooling system, pump; Battery, 12 volt 40 amp hr.

TRANSMISSION: Clutch, B. & B. dry three-plate; Gear box, four speeds, all synchromesh; Overall ratios, top, 3.73; 3rd, 4.75; 2nd, 6.14; 1st, 8.02; Final drive, hypoid bevel, ratio 3.73 to 1.

CHASSIS: Brakes, Girling disc front and rear; Disc dia, 11in front, 10in rear; Suspension, front, equal length wishbones and coil springs; rear, de Dion axle and coil springs; Dampers, Girling tele-

scopic; Wheels, Dunlop light alloy disc, bolt-on; Tyre size, front 6.00-16in; Rear 6.50-16in; Steering, rack and pinion; steering wheel, 15in dia Derrington light alloy, leather covered.

DIMENSIONS: Wheelbase, 7ft 5in (226 cm); Track, front, 4ft 2½in (128 cm); Rear, 4ft 4in (132 cm); Overall length, 12ft 11½in (395 cm); Overall width, 5ft 1in (155 cm); Overall height, 2ft 5in (74 cm) (to scuttle); Ground clearance, 3in (7.6 cm) (at sump); Weight, 1,904lb (865 kg); Weight distribution (dry), F. 48 per cent, R. 52 per cent.

PERFORMANCE: With gearing and wheel size as above, maximum at 5,800 r.p.m.; top gear, 135 m.p.h.; third gear, 104 m.p.h.; second gear, 81 m.p.h.; first gear, 62 m.p.h.; m.p.h. per 1,000 r.p.m., in top, 23; standing quarter mile, 13 sec; 0-100 m.p.h., 11 sec.

Small frontal area is comparable to many 1100-cc cars.

'58 **L**ister **J**aguar

Lower, lighter, faster and more in demand

Unusual appearing tail section covers large (45.6-gallon) fuel tank, spare tire, battery.

Clean design of body is evident. Height to top of cowl is 27 inches, top of windshield 33 inches, and headrest 39 inches.

BRIAN LISTER (Light Engineering Ltd., Abbey Road, Cambridge, England), offers an improved version of an already excellent sports-racing car for 1958. It is available in three versions: with Jaguar engine, Chevrolet V-8 engine or without an engine for those who would prefer to install something different.

Many detail changes were incorporated in the new car, but the most important were the enlargement of the Girling disc brakes (from 11 inches at front and 10 inches at rear to 12 inches all around) and a redesigned body.

Frontal area has been reduced by some 10% and now measures approximately 11½ square feet, which is as low as that of most British 1100-cc cars. The overall body thickness has been reduced by 3 inches, and the height to the cowl and headrest is 27 and 39 inches, respectively. A roll-over structure is incorporated into the headrest.

These changes in body design, coupled with a slight weight reduction and horsepower increases, should make the car capable of nearly 200 miles per hour (with the proper gearing, of course), according to the manufacturer.

The new tail design, in addition to aiding aerodynamics, also increases the fuel storage space. The 45-gallon fuel tank is located in the top area of the tail section, and the spare tire is mounted below the tank. The battery is mounted low in the tail, to the right of the spare wheel.

The Lister organization handles the design and construction of the chassis and the assembly of all the components, but the body panelwork is left to the capable firm of Williams and Pritchard Ltd., of Edmonton. Some of the Lister bodies are aluminum and some are magnesium alloy. No price difference is given for the two, but it can safely be assumed that the magnesium body will be more costly.

An indication of the popularity of and respect for the Lister-Jaguar is the order placed for one of the new cars by David Murray—"Le Patron" of the world-famous Ecurie Ecosse racing team (twice winners of the Le Mans 24-hour race in D-type Jaguars). It is expected that Archie Scott-Brown, who has done so well for Lister in the past, will drive for Ecurie Ecosse in certain events.

Three U.S. representatives have been established so far. Tom Carstens, of Seattle, will represent the states of Washington and Oregon and Northern California. Carroll Shelby of Dallas represents the balance of the area west of the Mississippi and Auto Engineering, Inc., Lexington, Mass., represents the Eastern seaboard. All have cars on order, and they are eagerly awaited by U.S. motoring enthusiasts. ◎

CHASSIS DETAILS

Frame	3-inch x 14G seamless drawn steel tubing
Brakes	*Girling disc, 12-inch diameter, front and rear
Suspension	Front, equal length wishbones and coil springs
	Rear, de Dion and coil springs
Shock absorbers	Girling telescopic
Wheels	Dunlop perforated disc, 5.00 x 16, light alloy, knock-off type
Tire size	Front, 6.00 x 16
	Rear, 6.50 x 16
Steering	Rack and pinion
Turns lock to lock	2
Steering wheel	Derrington light alloy, leather covered, 15-inch diameter

CHASSIS DIMENSIONS

Wheelbase	90.75 inches
Tread	52 inches front, 53.5 inches rear
Overall length	162 inches
Overall width	62.5 inches
Overall height	27 inches at cowl, 39 inches at headrest
Ground clearance	*4 inches at sump
Turning circle	40 feet
Dry weight	1736 pounds
Weight distribution, dry	48% front 52% rear
Tank capacity	45.6 U.S. gallons
Price, Jaguar engine	$7700
without engine	$4900

The above are factory delivered prices.
*Items are different from last year's car.

NEW YEAR LISTERS

INFLUENCE OF FRANK COSTIN BEGINS TO SHOW

Lister-Jaguar for 1959 has smooth profile synonymous with Costin body projects. Acetate cockpit canopy imparts an almost coupé look—and aerodynamic efficiency

A FEW weeks ago Frank Costin left the de Havilland Aircraft Company and joined Brian Lister at Cambridge to concentrate on car design. A fully qualified aerodynamicist his work has had great international influence on the shape of sports/racing and Grand Prix cars over the last few years.

He was mainly responsible for the splendid shape and ducting of the original streamlined Lotus—the mark 8 and has continued to advise on the profile of all subsequent Lotus cars including the Grand Prix models.

He was responsible for the highly efficient air-penetrating single-seater bodywork of the current-type Vanwall, and also designed an aerodynamic coupé for the fabulous 1957

Front of the new Lister has been considerably cleaned up but there is still a bonnet-top bulge to accommodate the vertically-installed Jaguar engine

Driver comfort has come in for close study with deep, soft leather bucket seats, well-rolled around the edges to provide maximum support. Twin S.U. fuel pumps are accessible by driver's door

Le Mans Maserati V8 which however the manufacturers ruined when they actually produced it.

The 1959 Lister-Jaguar is the first result of the teaming of Frank Costin with Brian Lister Ltd. as their Chief Designer. It is understandable that the first major change would be to body shape.

The bodywork of the 1959 Lister-Jaguars is, by modern standards, relatively conventional, embodying the results of lessons learnt over the years from previous designs and tests. The moulded screen/high tail arrangement is a logical development of the one originally designed by Costin for the class-winning Le Mans Lotus cars of 1957. This arrangement has since been used by various other manufacturers. A tonneau cover, which is the subject of a Patent and is essential to the whole conception, will be added later.

The photographs show the attention to overall cleanness at which the designer has aimed, the sole offending blister being necessary to accommodate the Jaguar engine. This excrescence, however, is made to serve also as a "convection release" of the underbonnet air. For various reasons it was decided not to place the engine on its side at this stage.

In all earlier designs Mr. Costin has made use of a fully ducted radiator: it is interesting to note, therefore, that this vehicle has merely an entry duct. It is possible that further developments may include ducting aft of the radiator.

Cold air is taken from the relatively static region to the rear of the front wheel well via the oil cooler and thence to the cockpit—the considerable depression in this latter being responsible for the cooling flow.

The inboard disc brakes at the rear are cooled by the method used so successfully on the Vanwall, in which the hot boundary layer of air is scraped from the disc while a considerable volume of cold air is closely ducted around it via a raised intake in the undertray. (Ducts and attachments for this system weigh less than 2 lb.) A duct around the finned rear cover serves to cool the Salisbury final drive unit.

The cockpit which by any standards is both roomy and comfortable is still the subject of detail testing and development and, in its final form, will be fully air-conditioned.

Another aspect of driver comfort in this latest car are the

Instrumentation is well over to left of cockpit to provide maximum room for driver. Gearbox is Moss/Jaguar and the light-alloy steering wheel has four spokes

SPECIFICATION

ENGINE
6-cylinder in line. Bore: 83 mm. Stroke: 106 mm. Capacity: 3,442 c.c. o.h.v. Compression ratio: 9 : 1. Three Twin-choke Webers. Power Output: 250 b.h.p. at 6,000 r.p.m. With 3-litre Jaguar engine, Bore: 83 mm. Stroke: 92 mm. Capacity 2,986 c.c. This can be equipped with the latest 35/40 head at an extra charge.

TRANSMISSION
Four speed. Ratios: Top 3.54 : 1. 3rd 4.525. 2nd 5.825. 1st 7.610.

SUSPENSION
Front: Equal length wishbones and coil springs. Rear: De Dion and coil springs. Girling telescopic dampers all round.

STEERING
Rack and pinion. 2 turns lock to lock. Turning circle 40 ft.

BRAKES
Dunlop disc. 12 in. diameter front and rear.

DIMENSIONS
Wheelbase 7ft. 6¾ in. Track (front) 4 ft. 4 in. (rear) 4 ft. 5½ in. Overall length 14 ft. 4¾ in. Overall width 5 ft. 7 in. Overall height 2 ft. 7 in. at scuttle. 3 ft. 2 in. overall. Ground clearance: 4½ in. Sump: 6 in. chassis: Dry weight 15½ cwt.

TANK CAPACITY
38 gallons (Imp.).

PERFORMANCE DATA
Top gear m.p.h. at 1,000 r.p.m. 24.
Weight distribution dry: Front 48 per cent. Rear, 52 per cent.

new specially designed seats which provide maximum support for high-speed cornering.

Frontal area is low for a vehicle of this engine capacity and, when coupled with the expected low drag coefficient, should yield maximum speeds in the region of 180 m.p.h. from 250 b.h.p. Equipped with the famous 3.8 litre 300 b.h.p. Jaguar engine for British and United States circuits this car should have an interesting performance. It is also available with the 3-litre Jaguar engine for Appendix "C" and Sports Car Championship races.

"Dick" Barton, Listers No. 1 racing mechanic, will accompany the cars to all meetings this year together with a team from the works. Don Moore, who has his own business in Cambridge, will be in charge of engine preparation and development.

Chassis details remain, at this stage, unchanged, with one important exception; for 1959 Dunlop disc brakes will be used. Therefore tyres, wheels and brakes on the 1959 Listers are now all made by the same organization.

Drivers for the works cars during 1959 will be Ivor Bueb and Bruce Halford. Other drivers may be added to the team from time to time, for instance, in long distance events such as the Le Mans 24 hours and the Nurburgring 1000 kilometres race.

This interesting body is the first of many developments (not all limited to motor cars) planned by Listers in association with Frank Costin.

Height of the tail fin is dictated by the greater height of the windscreen called for by the regulations

Jaguar New Competition Car

BRIGGS CUNNINGHAM'S PRIVATE ENTRY FOR LE MANS IS A LOGICAL DEVELOPMENT OF D-TYPE

BRITISH hopes for an outright win in the Le Mans 24-hour race, starting tomorrow, depend largely on the new competition Jaguar entered privately by American Briggs Cunningham. Jaguars have already five victories to their credit in the race, a record shared with Bentleys; of these outright wins two were achieved with cars privately entered by Ecurie Ecosse in 1956 and 1957.

This new car does not necessarily represent a try-out for future works entries. It is only natural for a company such as Jaguar, whose reputation has been enhanced by participation in racing, to continue development, even though they withdrew officially from competition at the end of the 1956 season. The position is that Briggs Cunningham has persuaded Sir William Lyons to place at his disposal one of the several models on which the company have continued development during the past five years. This new model is a logical development of the D-type, and probably represents the truest interpretation of the current regulations for open sports cars. In other words, Jaguar have designed a car to meet these

regulations from its inception rather than adapt existing models to meet the new requirements. Thus the shape and proportions of the body are dictated by the latest windscreen regulation (9·84in. vertical height of transparent material), and it has a streamline form designed to produce the minimum drag within this framework. Height of the scuttle, 2ft 10in., is very similar to that of the D-type, but the height to the top of the tail fin, 4ft 5¼in., is considerably greater, as is the overall length of 14ft 2in. compared with 12ft 10in. This latter dimension is greater for two reasons—the wheelbase, at 8ft 0in., is 6in. longer, and more length of body form behind the driver's head fairing was required to obtain an efficient streamline shape because of the higher windscreen. Front and rear tracks are equal at 4ft 0in.; the D-type had 4ft 0in. front track, but a 4ft 2in. rear track.

Laminated safety glass is used for the windscreen, which is curved and metalframed. With a screen of these proportions it is necessary for the driver to have vision through it, instead of over it, as was possible with the old regulations. It is, therefore, essential to have wipers

which will clear the screen when it becomes obscured, and work efficiently at very high speeds. A considerable amount of development work has been necessary to solve these problems. Lucas have evolved a special heavy-duty motor which operates at 100 strokes per minute (the same as the high speed range in a normal two-speed motor), and Trico have assisted in the development of the special blades and washing equipment. There are two water jets inside a deflector shield, and tests have proved these to work satisfactorily with direct jets on to the screen at speeds as high as 160 m.p.h. A reservoir tank containing a mixture of water and wood alcohol is located in the cockpit; adjacent to it is the wiper switch and operating plunger for the washing equipment.

From the engine bulkhead rearwards, a monocoque type of construction is used for the combined body-chassis unit. It is constructed entirely of aluminium alloy with riveted joints, and the outer panels are stressed members. Main load-carrying members are the scuttle structure, central backbone member and rear bulkhead-section. Within this rear bulkhead-

---

⎯⎯⎯⎯⎯⎯⎯⎯⎯ SPECIFICATION ⎯⎯⎯⎯⎯⎯⎯⎯⎯

ENGINE

No. of cylinders	6 in line
Bore and stroke	85 x 88mm (3·346 x 3·465in.)
Displacement	2,997 c.c. (183 cu. in.)
Valve position	Opposed in hemispherical combustion chamber; operated by 2 o.h.c.
Compression ratio	10·0 to 1
Max. b.h.p. (net)	295 at 6,800 r.p.m.
Carburation	Lucas port-type fuel injection
Fuel pump	Lucas
Tank capacity	26·5 Imp. gallons (120·5 litres)
Oil tank capacity	3·5 Imp. gallons (15·9 litres)
Oil filter	Full flow
Cooling system	Pressurized, pump without fan
Battery	12 volt, 48 amp. hr. Lucas lightweight

TRANSMISSION

Clutch	Borg and Beck 7·25in. dia triple plate
Gearbox	Four speeds, synchromesh on all ratios, central gear lever
Overall gear ratios	Top 3·31; 3rd 4·23; 2nd 5·44; 1st 7·10
Final drive	Hypoid bevel, ratio 3·31 to 1

CHASSIS

Brakes	12in. dia non-servo Dunlop discs (inboard at rear) with 2 segmental pads per disc
Suspension: front	Independent wishbones and torsion bar
rear	Independent wishbones with 2 combined telescopic dampers and coil springs per wheel
Dampers	Girling telescopic
Wheels	Dunlop alloy with centre lock hubs
Tyre size	6·50 x 16 Dunlop Stabilia (low silhouette)
Steering	Rack and pinion
No. of turns lock to lock	2·5

DIMENSIONS
(Manufacturer's figures)

Wheelbase	8ft 0in. (243·8 cm)
Track	4ft 0in. (121·9 cm)
Overall length	14ft 2in. (431·8 cm)
Overall width	5ft 2·75in. (159·4 cm)
Overall height	4ft 5·25in. (135·2 cm) to fin, 3ft 8·75in. (113·7 cm) to screen
Ground clearance	6·5in. (16·5 cm)
Turning circle	38ft 4·5in. (11·7 m)
Kerb weight	17·2 cwt (1,925 lb) (872 Kg) (estimated)

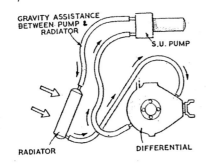

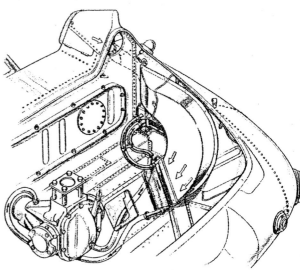

The driver can bring into circuit an oil cooler when the oil temperature of the chassis-mounted final drive unit reaches a predetermined figure. The oil is circulated by a S.U. fuel pump, as shown in the circuit diagram on the left

section is housed the I.C.I. flexible rubber-and-fabric fuel tank, which has a capacity of 26·5 gallons. It is clipped to the constraining framework at several points to avoid complete collapse as the fuel is used. With fuel injection—Lucas port-type is used on this engine—it is important that air is kept out of the fuel system. To achieve this object, two anti-surge pots are fitted at each side of the tank, to avoid risk of fuel starvation during severe cornering either to the right or left. There is a fuel feed pipe from the bottom of each of these anti-surge pots to the inlet side of the continuously running fuel booster pump, which is electrically driven and operates at 100 p.s.i.; surplus fuel is returned to the tank. The effect of these anti-surge pots and baffling is so effective that in racing conditions the fuel can be used to within the last three pints of the tank capacity without starvation.

The fin section of the tail is hinged at one side to provide access to the horizontally mounted spare wheel and to the compulsory luggage space above it, which must be able to contain a trunk measuring 25·6 × 15·75 × 7·875in.

As on the production series D-types, there is a front sub-frame on which the front suspension, steering and engine are mounted. This is bolted to the bulkhead

of the monocoque structure, and is constructed largely of square-section steel tubes. For access to the engine bay, a one-piece light alloy nose cowl containing lamps and cooling ducts is hinged at its lower forward edge.

Most interesting technical innovation is the new independent rear suspension. The Salisbury hypoid bevel final drive unit is mounted directly to the chassis, with fixed length universal drive shafts to each wheel; these act also as the upper arms of the wishbone linkages. Main loads are absorbed in a massive wishbone arm of fabricated box section steel, with widely based pivots attached to a separate small sub-frame. Because of the stiff section of this lower arm and the spread of the mounting points, there is no need for any other type of torque stay or radius arm. The outer end of each wishbone is pivoted to an aluminium housing, inside of which are two opposed taper roller bearings for the wheel hub. There are two suspension units, consisting of a Girling telescopic damper surrounded by a coil spring, for each wheel. They are mounted, one at either side of the drive shaft, to the common transverse pivot pin in the lower wishbone. From the forward mounting of each damper unit there is also a drop link connecting to a transverse anti-roll bar.

The Dunlop disc brakes are mounted inboard at the rear. This confers a big advantage in the reduction of unsprung weight, but involved some severe problems during development of the car. It is more difficult to get rid of the generated heat during severe braking when they are mounted inboard, compared with the more usual position at the wheels. Two separate systems are provided for cooling the brakes. Projecting below the otherwise clean under-shield are two ducts to direct cooling air on to the forward and open sides of the discs. In addition, there is an entry duct above each wheel fairing, through which cooling air is directed with a reverse flow on to the rear-mounted calipers. In spite of this provision, it was found that a great deal of heat was being transferred inwards from the discs, through the drive shaft flanges to the lubricating oil of the final drive unit. The normal type of rubber or leather oil seals at the output flanges were found to be ineffective, and special silicone types were developed. In addition, an oil cooler can be brought into circuit by the driver when the oil temperature approaches a critical stage, such as might occur after severe and sustained braking. A normal S.U. type of fuel pump circulates oil through a cooler which is situated in a by-pass from the

Left: Oil tank, showing the methods used for de-aerating. On the inlet side there is a fish-tail diffuser which leads the oil to a small weir, at which stage the air is separated out in the breather compartment. Further de-aeration is achieved as the oil passes over the drilled baffle plate above the static oil level. Right: Corner section of the windscreen, with the special highspeed wiper, the two water jets and a directional baffle plate, which also prevents the jets being blocked with flies or dirt

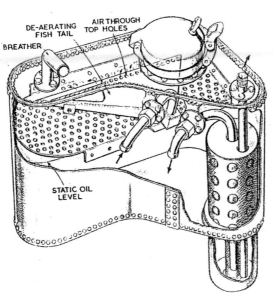

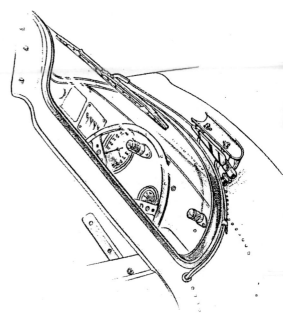

JAGUAR
NEW COMPETITION
CAR . . .

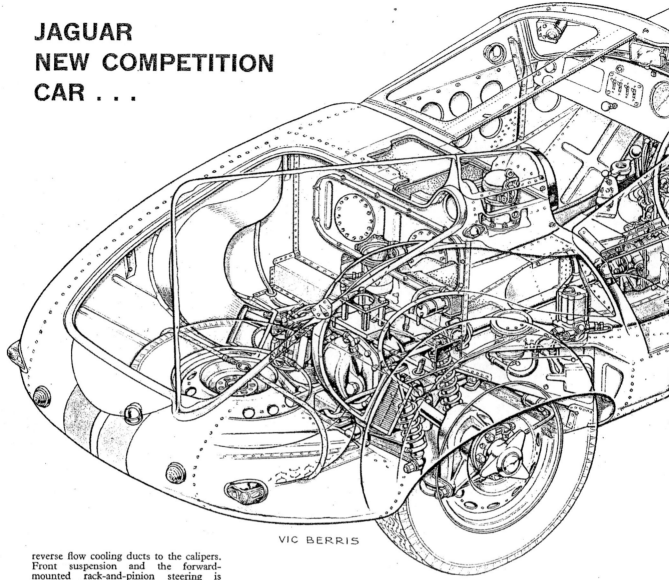

VIC BERRIS

reverse flow cooling ducts to the calipers. Front suspension and the forward-mounted rack-and-pinion steering is basically the same as on the earlier D-type, with detail improvement and changes in geometry to improve road-holding. The wishbones are steel forgings with ball pivots top and bottom, and incorporate an anti-roll bar. Among the improvements is a saving of 11lb on the unsprung weight of each assembly.

Since the car appeared at the official practice day on 9 April a tail fin has been added. This not only improved directional stability at high speed but enabled another 300 r.p.m. to be obtained in top gear by splitting the air flow across the tail and reducing turbulence. Above the passenger's seat there is a transparent plastic tonneau cover.

Among the new developments on the otherwise basically unchanged and well-known overhead camshaft engine is the use of an aluminium cylinder block and

Left: The bulges aft of the doors are air scoops for brake cooling. Right: A feature is the air intake in the nose, flanked by faired head lamps. Colour scheme is the American medium blue on white. The special windscreen washer shield is forward of the steering wheel

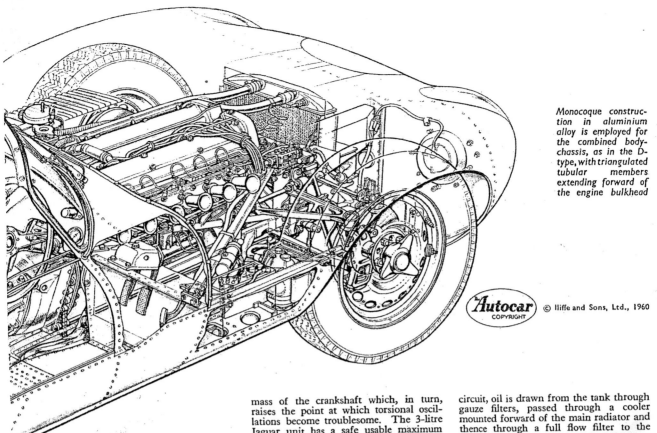

Autocar COPYRIGHT © Iliffe and Sons, Ltd., 1960

crankcase with pressed-in dry-type cast-iron liners for the bores, as used on previous 3-litre versions of this engine, with bores of 85mm and strokes of 88mm.

In the version used on the 9 April practice day, titanium connecting rods were used. In its pure form titanium has an ultimate tensile strength of 30 tons per square inch but when alloyed with aluminium and magnesium, and depending on its heat treatment, this figure can be increased to 70 tons per square inch. Its main advantage is that its unit weight is only half that of steel. When used for connecting rods this reduces considerably the reciprocating weight and rotational

mass of the crankshaft which, in turn, raises the point at which torsional oscillations become troublesome. The 3-litre Jaguar unit has a safe usable maximum speed of 7,000 r.p.m., maximum peak power of 295 b.h.p. being developed at 6,800 r.p.m.

The light-alloy cylinder head, with valves operated directly by two overhead camshafts and inverted tappets, is a development of the previous 30-40 competition units—indicating that the inlet valves are placed at 30deg and the exhausts at 40deg from the vertical axis. Carburation is by the Lucas port-type fuel injection sytem with gate-type throttle valves, as described in *The Autocar* of 9 November 1956. The one change from this earlier development is the use of a single-shuttle metering distributor.

The oil system is, of course, on the dry sump principle, with one pressure and two scavenge pumps which feed direct to the oil tank mounted just forward of the chassis bulkhead. On the pressure

circuit, oil is drawn from the tank through gauze filters, passed through a cooler mounted forward of the main radiator and thence through a full flow filter to the crankcase gallery.

The gearbox, mounted in unit with the engine, has synchromesh on all forward ratios, as had earlier competition types. There is, however, no longer a Plessey pump to supply hydraulic servo assistance for the disc brakes; acceptable pedal loads have been obtained without the use of servo assistance. To comply with the Le Mans regulations, front and rear systems are operated from independent hydraulic circuits. This is achieved by the use of a tandem type of master cylinder in which the operating pistons abut mechanically in the event of an hydraulic failure in one of the independent circuits.

Over a timed section of the Sarthe circuit during the official practice day, this new Jaguar was faster than any of its rivals. If it performs reliably for 24 hours it could be the overall winner.

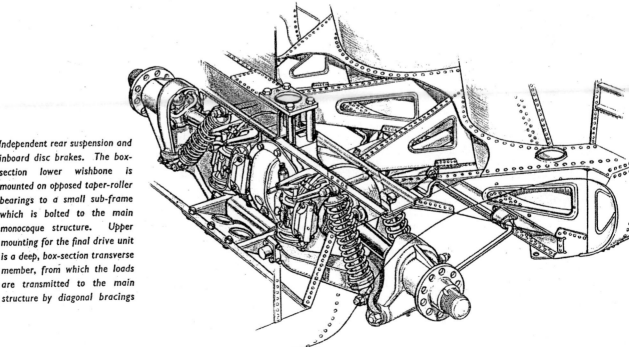

Independent rear suspension and inboard disc brakes. The box-section lower wishbone is mounted on opposed taper-roller bearings to a small sub-frame which is bolted to the main monocoque structure. Upper mounting for the final drive unit is a deep, box-section transverse member, from which the loads are transmitted to the main structure by diagonal bracings

JAGUAR-POWERED SPORTS CARS

Remembering the good old days

WE ALL KNOW Jaguar's 6-cylinder XK engine made its name with five Le Mans wins. We know they used the classic C-Types and D-Types to do so, but they were not alone in using that smooth and powerful twincam unit. During the mid-Fifties, four small British companies produced Jaguar-engine sports racers which could often out-perform their thoroughbred cousins from Coventry. Their shattering performances on the road, as recorded in 20-year-old test figures, make some modern exotics look sad.

HWM, Cooper, Tojeiro and Lister built and raced these cars with varying degrees of success. Hersham & Walton Motors (HWM) and Brian Lister (Light Engineering) Ltd chose simple twin-tube chassis for their designs while the Cooper Car Company and Tojeiro Automotive Developments preferred multitubular space frames; the simpler solution proved more effective.

Unusual for racing history, it's possible to pin down the start of this story: August 11, 1951 at England's Boreham Airfield circuit. It was high summer so it was gray, cold and raining when the West Essex Car Club ran their *Daily Mail* race meeting. The soaked crowd had seen today's Brabham boss Bernie Ecclestone spin away his chances in the Formula 3 heats and then watched Brian Shawe-Taylor's ERA win the 15-lap feature. Splashing home in 4th place was George Abecassis, a partner in Hersham & Walton

Motors, in one of his own HWMs. It was a makeshift car, it was stuck in top gear and he had only one thought to console himself. It handled well. "This," he thought, blowing away raindrops which streamed from his visor, "would make a damned fine sports car." Just behind him ran an engine trader from London named Oscar Moore. He was in an older HWM and was thinking much the same.

Moore had had a poor season with the unreliable Alta 2-liter in his HWM and his sons Peter and Terry recall his problems with the Alta exhaust which persistently fell apart. Eventually he fed the manifolding directly into a hole cut in one chassis tube. "Now bloody well fall off," he yelled at it. It stayed put. Moore took his 1950 HWM back to his auto rental business and immediately began fitting an XK-120 engine for 1952. Eventually he and his mechanic Stan Harding delved into the unknown and bored out their 3442-cc XK engine to a full 3814 cc. Coincidentally, Richie Ginther was sucking his teeth and doing likewise to an XK block for Phil Hill. It was the start of the 3.8 Jaguar story.

Moore's car was obsoleted in 1953 as C-Type Jags filtered into club racing, but he had been successful enough to convince Abecassis to try a Jag engine in a factory HWM. He started with a spare HWM single-seater chassis with torsion-bar De Dion rear suspension and transverse leaf front setup. He bought a lovely

The second series HWM is seen at the left and this is the type in which John Heath was killed at the Mille Miglia. Above is the original HWM-Jaguar, driven by George Abecassis at Oulton Park.

At the left is your classic Lister-Jaguar photo, with Stirling Moss manhandling the car to victory in the sports car race prior to the 1958 British Grand Prix. Below is the HWM in its ultimate form, here with George Abecassis leading a C-Type Jaguar at Goodwood in 1956.

bodyshell originally meant for a Jaguar-engine Alta hillclimb car, added a 3.4-liter XK engine and produced HWM 1, the first works HWM-Jaguar sports racing car.

This drum-brake bombshell had more than 240 bhp on tap as a result of Abecassis's partner John Heath's pioneering adaptation of triple Weber carburetion for the XK engine. Harry Weslake developed suitable camshafts and the car started on several promising performances in sprints and long-distance events.

For 1954 Abecassis and Heath decided to drop their open-wheel activities and stick to sports cars. Two more of the Jag-engine cars were built, using MG-derived coil spring front suspensions, and sold to customers, one for street use. Old HWM 1 was rebodied with a steel shell to withstand the 1954 Mille Miglia. Abecassis wanted a passenger, "because it's lonely down in the south if you get stranded," and Denis Jenkinson jumped at the chance. Jenks, who had never been above 110 mph in his life, recalls Abecassis demonstrating the car to him on an *Autostrada*, where he went straight to 150 mph and held it on the way to Count Maggi's "for tea." The car broke after 150 miles of the race, but a year later Jenks returned with Stirling Moss in the Mercedes and they won.

Abecassis raced HWM 1 extensively through 1954 and scored a fine 2nd place behind Gonzales' big 4.9 Ferrari and ahead of the works Jaguars and Aston Martins at Silverstone. Then the car was sold to hillclimber Ray Fielding. All-coil-spring cars were built for 1955 and 1956, but John Heath died in the Mille Miglia in the 1956 car and his death robbed HWM and Abecassis of much of their reason to go racing. When George retired, HWM also left the scene.

Two more HWM-Jaguars were built in 1956, one on an Alta Formula 2 chassis and the other a striking coupe road car. In the same year, Tony Gaze raced one of the 1954 coil spring cars down

under where he won the Wigram sports car race in New Zealand despite a hair-raising Le Mans start. Reg Parnell walked over to him as they lined up opposite their cars, winked and said, "I've put her in gear for you." Gaze sprinted to his car, fired it up and promptly departed in reverse through the pit counter. He sold the car and heard it had been destroyed in a road accident which killed the mechanic driving it. Two years ago, Gaze, farming in the west of England, was amazed to receive a parking ticket traced to him from the HWM. He hadn't seen the car for 20 years.

John Cooper followed HWM's lead in 1954 when wealthy private owner Peter Whitehead asked him to build a lightweight C-Type. Whitehead had won Le Mans for Jaguar in 1951 and had been racing an F2 Cooper-Alta in 1953. The Surbiton concern had never used such a large and powerful engine as the Jaguar, and Owen "The Beard" Maddock drew a new multi-tubular space frame under John's direction. He felt there was a good chance of attracting other customers and invested in a special magnesium final-drive casing to accept an ENV nosepiece. This allowed an independent rear end, and interested Bill Heynes of Jaguar who was toying with irs for his works cars.

The chassis was a massive affair using 1.5-in. diameter steel tube bent into typical Cooper ellipses in defiance of "good engineering practice." Double wishbones relieved the transverse leaf springs of the location duty they performed on all preceding Cooper models, and John adopted an unusual Porsche-like bodyshell with the radiator laid flat above a shark-mouth intake below the nose. He hoped it would yield a 10-15 mph top speed bonus but today recalls ". . . that comical system. I tested it on the Dorking By-pass but it got hotter and hotter and each time we had to make the radiator bigger and bigger until finally we gave up and mounted it behind a proper hole like everybody else."

At the left is the Cooper-Jaguar built for Peter Whitehead, who also owned the Ferrari in our October 1977 Salon section. Labeled the T33, it was modestly successful, but the closed Porsche-type nose had to be opened up, as you can see below with Whitehead driving the car in its final form.

Jack Brabham was on the list of drivers who raced the second Tojeiro-Jaguar (left), one that sponsor John Ogier personally destroyed in a sprint event. Ivor Bueb (above) in the first Tojeiro-Jaguar built for Ecurie Ecosse, a car which was bent and rebuilt, but later destroyed when its brakes failed while Masten Gregory was driving it at Goodwood (right).

Whitehead's new Cooper-Jaguar T33 made a wet and not very impressive debut in the 1954 International Trophy Silverstone meeting. It later enjoyed modest success, registered UBH 292 and its new Dunlop disc-brake system paid off in humbling some good opposition. At a time when the whole car sold for around £4000, the brakes alone cost £750.

Two more of the pan-lid styled Mark Is were produced for a couple of northern enthusiasts named Jack Walton and Bertie Bradnack, but in January 1955 a much-improved T38 Cooper-Jaguar Mark II was displayed at the Brussels Motor Show. It had a full D-Type dry-sump engine mounted further back in the frame and inclined 8 degrees from vertical. This allowed a lower and more handsome nose line, blended in to a far more handsome and conventional bodyshell. This prototype replaced Peter Whitehead's Mark I and was subsequently taken down to Australia by him and sold to the late Stan Jones.

A second Mark II was ordered by Tommy Sopwith, son of the Hawker aircraft chief, and his aviation connections led John Cooper on many visits to Blackburn Aviation which was developing a Turbomeca gas turbine power unit. Sopwith wanted to race a turbocar (remember this was 1955) but development was so slow he settled for Jaguar power instead. His midnight blue Cooper-Jag became one of the most successful of its type. The

third and last Mark II was completed, road-equipped, for Col Michael Head. It was smaller, lower and more svelte than its sisters and Col Head clocked thousands of road miles driving it to race meetings in Scandinavia and the U.K.

While HWM and Cooper showed the way, Tojeiro and Lister took the Jaguar-engine sports racing theme to its ultimate conclusion in 1959. Both marques shared common roots. John Tojeiro and Brian Lister both lived in Cambridge and both began racing around 1950. John Toj drove a lightweight-body MG TA while Lister progressed from Morgan 4/4s to Cooper-MGs. When John decided to build a better-handling chassis around his MG's engine he handcrafted his own twin-tube frame, working in a tiny shed at Little Gransden just outside the city. Some friends ordered replicas before the prototype was complete, and John had some parts made for him by the long-established specialist engineering company of Geo Lister & Sons, Abbey Road, Cambridge. Brian's father Horace was one of the "Sons" and when his parents retired in 1954 Brian and his brother Raymond became joint managing directors—as they are today.

Tojeiro next built a 2-liter Bristol-engine car that looked like a Ferrari Barchetta and became the base for the production AC Ace. It also impressed John Ogier, a prosperous farmer who raced a black XK-120 which he felt had an obsolete chassis

An early Lister-Jaguar (above) at Aintree with Archie Scott-Brown driving, 1957. Brown was famous for his heroic driving style despite having only one arm, and died later at Spa while racing a Lister.

putting on opposite lock. "I'm not used to your body," it said. On another occasion, Gammon knew his communicant really was Mike Hawthorn because the woman medium blushed and said, "He's just said something which I won't repeat on a Sunday, and certainly not in church!" All of which is sensational stuff but, unfortunately, a cog* has slipped somewhere because this was 1957. Mike had 18 months and a World Championship left to him.

Late in October 1957 Ogier wrote off the wire-wheel car and the original 7 GNO was sold to Frank Cantwell in New Zealand. Tojeiro was now without a works car. John Toj was developing works ACs for Le Mans and when David Murray ordered a car for Ecurie Ecosse he had to wait until July 1958 for delivery. There Ivor Bueb debuted an extraordinarily pretty new Tojeiro Jaguar to place 4th behind Moss's winning Lister-Jag. They were split by little works Lotuses, one of which equaled Moss's fastest lap. The writing was on the wall for the big-engine car.

Ecurie Ecosse achieved success with their new Tojeiro-Jaguar when Ron Flockhart drove it at Goodwood on Easter Monday 1959, and a second car was ordered specifically for Le Mans. Flockhart bent the original car in the Nürburgring 1000 km and it was returned to Ogier before the new car, with a tail-finned headrest à la D-Type made its debut with a "square" 86 mm x 86 mm 3-liter engine at Le Mans. Flockhart shared it with Jock Lawrence and they headed the start lineup, outlasted the other Jaguar-powered cars and then dropped out with a warped cylinder head early on Sunday morning.

Jimmy Clark shared this car with Masten Gregory in the RAC Tourist Trophy at Goodwood. Entering Woodcote Corner the bass-voiced little Kansan found its brakes had gone away. He stood up in the cockpit as the car streaked for the safety bank and was thrown high over it as the Tojeiro broke its back and folded into a smoldering Vee on impact. Gregory was picked up with a broken shoulder and in shock. Eventually, the original Ecurie Ecosse car was sold to the Lewis brothers for sprints and hillclimbs, and in 1963 Mrs Vivienne Lewis crashed it and was killed during the Brighton Speed Trials. It was a tragic end to an accident-punctuated story. Today John Tojeiro runs a plastics company.

Meanwhile Lister had gone from strength to strength. I can't detail the MG, Bristol and Maserati-engine Listers here, but briefly the story began in 1953 when Brian Lister decided racing a car bearing another's name was an opportunity missed. He persuaded his father to allocate £1500 to build a company car and was allowed six months to get it running. With Archie Scott-Brown at the wheel, the MG-engine car won on its debut at Snetterton early in 1954. Brian remembers, "Father saw the race on TV and couldn't credit the times our company name was mentioned!" From then on he approved of Brian's racing which, for insurance purposes, Brian conducted under his own company name.

In 1956, a London jeweler named Norman Hillwood bought a Lister chassis intended for a Bristol engine and in March it was completed with a wet-sump Jaguar engine on SU carbs mated to a C-Type gearbox. Brian Lister knew this car was being built. He was contracted to BP Oil and the Shell-backed Jaguar works team had at that time just disbanded. Shell-BP needed a big sports car to combat Esso's Aston Martin and Ecurie Ecosse Jaguar teams and Bryan Turle of BP pressured Lister to build a Jaguar-engine big-banger. Brian wasn't convinced, as he wanted to go into F2. On reflection he decided the U.S. market might be lucrative and so bought his first dry-sump 3.4-liter D-Type engine from Jaguar at Coventry. An older chassis was reworked to accept it and a bodyshell based on Goldie Gardner's then-current record car was fitted. The end product was a projectile which packed 250 bhp into less than 1650 lb and Archie Scott-Brown drove it in his spectacular ragged-edge style to win 12 of his 14 races that year.

The first private Lister-Jaguar to leave Abbey Road was delivered that season to Dick Walsh of Torquay. It had a unique and neat bodyshell and it was to become one of the most famous Listers of all, driven by Bruce Halford and later by a youthful Jim Clark, among others.

handicapping a reliable and powerful engine. He discussed the problem with Tojeiro and readily agreed to sponsor a lightweight D-Type eater. The first Ogier-sponsored car was built in time for the late races of 1956, first with a C-Type engine and then with a 250-bhp D-Type engine to form the Tojeiro-Jaguar Mark II. The car had disc brakes, with the rears inboard in a De Dion axle arrangement. The brakes were non-servo and the car proved a beast to handle, threatening to snap into lurid oversteer at the slightest provocation while the brakes did not give confidence. Ogier—today chairman of Ogle Design (stylists of the Reliant Scimitar, etc)—tested the car and quickly discovered he was "too old for that type of car" and brought in another driver.

A second Tojeiro-Jaguar, with a 3-in. longer wheelbase, narrower track, lighter body and wire wheels instead of its forerunner's Dunlop disc type, was built for 1957. Drivers that season included Jack Brabham, Jack Fairman, Graham Hill and a good English club racer named Peter Gammon. He has the most extraordinary recollections of his Tojeiro drives: "I was sufficiently mediumistic to be put into a trance by the spirit of Mike Hawthorn while I was racing. He took over my body on at least two occasions and controlled moments I had which could have been really nasty accidents." On one of these occasions Mike's spirit voice apologized to Gammon for ricking his arm while

The first customer Lister-Jaguar (above, left) being raced at Le Mans. Above is the Mike Costin-designed Lister, which has a very intricate and expensive space frame (left). The frame shown is that of the last Lister built and for 1963 it received a full Costin coupe body (below) for Le Mans, but the car retired early with clutch problems.

During the winter of 1957–1958 Lister battled to fulfill a flood of orders. Briggs Cunningham brought three Listers to the States, two fitted with D-Type engines at Cambridge and the other bare to accept a Chevy V-8. Walt Hansgen was Cunningham's lead driver, and he won the SCCA Championship in 1958 and 1959 with these Alfred Momo-prepared cars. Momo, Carroll Shelby/ Jim Hall and Kjell Qvale were U.S. Lister agents and between them they brought in as many as 30 chassis. Some had Jaguar engines installed, others were shipped bare to accept American— usually Chevrolet—V-8s and one was completed in the U.S. with a Maserati V-8 unit.

For 1958 the cars were revised to full Appendix C trim with a humped hood like an elephant seal's trunk preceding a dropped scuttle line which allowed a regulation height windscreen to be accommodated within a small frontal area. A massive 38-gal. gas tank wrapped over the rear axle and was enclosed in a raised and bulbous tail.

Cunningham's Listers ran at Sebring and the organizers accepted Scott-Brown even though he had only one whole arm. His car blew up and was run over from behind by another which actually left a tire mark on his helmet.

Scott-Brown began the year in his usual winning style but after 14 months of nonstop racing Brian believes the little man was tired. At Silverstone in May new unscrubbed tires handicapped him and he was convincingly beaten by Masten Gregory in the new Ecosse Lister-Jaguar. It was the first time Archie had been beaten in one of his own cars, and he went to the Coupe de Spa at Francorchamps determined to avenge himself in the first Continental race for which he had been accepted.

The merciless battle between Archie and Gregory is history now, as is the brief rain shower which damped Seaman Corner up behind the clubhouse, the wild slide which the little Scot couldn't correct and the roll-over crash and burn which inflicted fatal injuries on this indomitable character.

Brian Lister was shattered, but he had commitments to fulfill and was persuaded that Archie wouldn't have wanted him to give up. Ecurie Ecosse built a special single-seater Lister for the Two

Worlds track race at Monza but in open-wheel trim it proved slower than their D-Types run there the previous year.

Brian wanted to win Le Mans, and employed aerodynamicist Frank Costin—of Lotus and Vanwall fame—to develop a new bodyshell for the existing chassis and an all-new space frame design to replace them. The 1959 Costin bodies were bulbous monstrosities compared to Lister's earlier functional elegance. At Le Mans the Ivor Bueb/Halford and Hansgen/Crawford cars threw rods before dawn as the 3-liter version of Jaguar's XK engine objected to its shortened stroke.

In July, "Ivor the Driver" crashed his Cooper in the Clermont F2 race and died a few days later. Brian was at Brands Hatch that day where Peter Blond crashed one of his works cars. Driving home he heard on his car radio of Jean Behra's death at Avus. At home he had a telephone call from Ivor's girl to tell him Ivor had died. At that instant Brian Lister retired from motor racing.

Today Mr Brian, as he is known in his modern Lister works, reflects: "You had to live motor racing to succeed in it and now I felt I had to build up our original business. Racing had always been a way of advertising our engineering skills and if we weren't careful it could become a profit absorber and destroy the parent company it had been intended to promote." The Costin space frame had proved prohibitively expensive to develop, concentration on Le Mans had proved expensive and the future for big-engine sports racers in general seemed bleak. It was time to go, and Lister-Jaguars became club racers before the passage of time turned them into the sought-after historic sports car classics they have become today. The solitary space frame chassis ran at Le Mans in 1963 under a Costin coupe bodyshell, owned and driven by London stockbrokers Peter Sargent and Peter Lumsden. It retired after the first pit stop when its clutch—wrongly assembled by the makers—sheared its bolts.

Talking of his products' latest successes in historic events Lister admits he is "very proud they have lasted so well" and as he drives through the University City in his bronze Rolls-Royce Silver Shadow with its dignified BRDC badge, it is obvious that he was one man who got his sums right.

Lister Jaguar

AS can be seen from our heading picture the alliance of aerodynamic expert Frank Costin and our old friend Brian Lister has resulted in a particularly attractive sports racing car. The Costin-designed body is completely new, is the same height as previous Listers and, with the wheels enclosed almost to hub level and the tail raised to the height of the windscreen, its low-drag qualities are obvious.

The chassis is exactly similar to last year with its ladder-type tubular frame but the disc brakes are by Dunlop, as are the tyres and the centre-lock wheels. Front suspension is by equal length wishbones and helical springs; at

Cockpit layout is most workmanlike and two very comfortable seats have been designed by Cox & Co. (Watford) Ltd.

the rear there's a de Dion axle and both units have telescopic dampers by Girling. It is interesting to note that the inboard rear disc brakes are cooled in similar manner to those of the Vanwall. A system of close-fitting ducting scrapes the hot air from the discs while cold air is fed through an intake in the under-tray.

The previous hump in the bonnet has disappeared and there is now only a small blister to clear the cam covers. This blister is open at the end facing the driver and makes up for the fact that although the radiator has a ducted entry there is no outlet arrangement. Outlet air escapes via the front wheel wells and through the port behind the blister. A good deal of attention has been paid to driver comfort and besides new and luxurious seating it is planned to have the cockpit fully air-conditioned.

The car is available with the 3½ litre Jaguar engine or with the 3.8 litre version. With the 3½ litre unit and its 250 b.h.p. there is a guarantee of 180 m.p.h. but no figures are quoted for the 300 brake horses of the 3.8 litre engine. For World Championship events Brian Lister will, of course, use the 2,986 c.c. Jaguar engine which can be equipped with the latest 35/40 head and may give power figures in excess even of those quoted for the 3½ litre unit.

The new Lister Jaguar has a four speed gearbox, the steering is by rack and pinion and it goes from lock to lock in two turns. The steering wheel is of light alloy with a wood rim and is made by Derringtons. Wheelbase of the car is 7 feet 6¼ inches and the overall length 14 feet 4¼ inches. The overall width is 5 feet 7 inches, height is 3 feet 2 inches and the turning circle is 40 feet. We can well imagine how its attractive appearance would have delighted the man whose alliance with Brian Lister first brought them both to eminence and somehow the stable is not quite the same without that fine Scots driver, the late Archie Scott Brown. However, Brian Lister has two grand drivers in Bruce Halford and Ivor Bueb and he will have others to handle cars in such events as Le Mans and the 1,000 kilometre race at the Nurburgring for he has his eye on the world championship for sports cars. The first of these new cars will take part in the Easter meeting at Goodwood and, thereafter, there will be privately owned cars, as well as works vehicles, at the many meetings to come. It may be that a privately owned car will be the first to chalk up a victory for Briggs Cunningham hopes to run one at Sebring on March 12.

View that many competitors will get of the new car. There is a boot in the car's shapely tail which will take one suitcase along with the spare wheel

When it comes to a fast, flat circuit the D-Type Jaguar is the car to beat. On tight U.S. circuits, modifications are in order. Here is the story.

SCI

Technical Report:

the

AFTER its postwar resumption in 1949, the 24-hour race at Le Mans has grown in stature annually, and among the first to realize its great publicity value was Jaguar Cars, Ltd. The fast-growing English firm has fielded by far the most successful team at Le Mans since the war, having won every other year since 1951. All their efforts have been concentrated on this classic, and entries in other races have been at best token efforts. Naturally and without question, the Jaguar competition cars are "Le Mans cars," perfectly suited to the fast, flat Sarthe circuit.

Though restricted in its original intent to the Le Mans type circuits, the D-Type Jag has been proven to be a car to beat on many courses. Production versions are now being distributed to individuals and racing stables, and certain faults are coming to light and being corrected, as we will see here.

From the body design standpoint, Reid Railton's 1938 design for the late John Cobb's land speed record car is the initial inspiration for the D-Type. Railton knew that many very fast cars were particularly sensitive to side winds at speed, and that designers had tried to move the center of

Balanced by bolt-on weights, the alloy wheels are reinforced by steel center sections. Dunlop-made wheels, tires and brakes are shrouded by contoured fender.

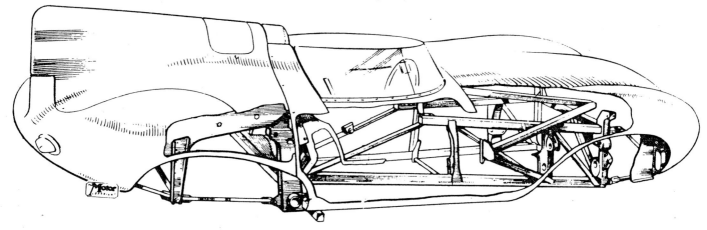

Steel is used for the production D-Type frame, which can be detached from the cockpit unit.

Drawing courtesy The Motor, England

hottest jaguar

pressure back by using fins. These early cars, though, were slab-sided as barns, and presented a lot of resistance to a lateral breeze. Railton took the cue and came up with a car that was aerodynamically clean from *all* directions, and sat flat at 400 mph with no finning.

In the U.S., Lee Chapel and Harold Post followed up with similar contours for Bonneville streamliners; another internationally significant design was the "Disco Volante," produced by collaboration between Alfa Romeo and Touring. These startling cars were introduced in June of 1952, and produced much more publicity than race wins. Jaguar saw the light, though, and by June of 1953 they had a prototype body ready for the C-Type that embodied the same basic streamlined ovoid-form-plus-wheel-bulges that the above cars had, and was clearly the daddy of the D.

Jag raced the older C body at Le Mans in '53, but they took the prototype C to the Jabbeke Highway in October of that year, and cranked it up to 178.383 mph with a basic M-Type engine. Development continued, and early May of 1954 found that C prototype (now fuel-injected) and a brand-new D Type on trial at Le Mans. Rolt circulated in the unpainted D some 2¼ mph faster than Ascari's 1953 4.5 Ferrari record, but at the end of the race itself he and Hamilton were 2.54 miles down on the rapid new 4.9 Ferrari. A later win in the Rheims 12-Hour made up for this.

The 1954 D-Types were true prototypes, and differed from the present production D in several respects. After a review of these differences, we can get on to a study of the present production car.

Frame construction was the main variation. Then, as now, the central cockpit was an oval-sectioned monocoque

Crankcase breather, ducted to oil tank, is shielded from exhaust heat. Wiring and other breathers have flexible armor.

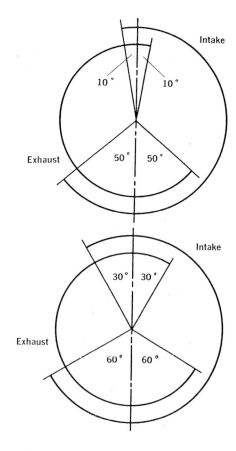

Engine inclination was necessary to provide room for carburetors and cold air box. Weber carbs receive fuel in series.

Upper diagram shows valve timing for stock Jaguar; duration is 240 degrees. Lower diagram illustrates the hotter timing and 270 degree duration of D.

unit, with a riveted 18-gauge aluminum-magnesium alloy stressed skin. In the 1954 car, though, the forward tubing structure for engine and front suspension support was made of a similar alloy, argon arc-welded to each other and to the cockpit. This was costly and time-consuming, and made repairs very difficult, as Colin Chapman also discovered with his prototype Mark VIII Lotus. Similarly, the radiators were borne by an extension of the main frame, and certain tubes in the center of the cockpit restricted the driver's elbow action.

Other differences include a non-synchromesh-low gearbox, an unnecessarily complex cooling system header tank and pressure valve, and lateral locating arms bolted and not welded to the rear axle tubes.

By the approach of 1955, the production version was taking shape, but not by any means soon enough for Briggs Cunningham to have one at Sebring in March. Walters and Hawthorn drove a 1954 factory car there, as did Duncan Hamilton in many European events. Le Mans 1955 saw the first production cars in action, but with certain additional prototype modifications. One of these cars duly won the race, but under admittedly inconclusive circumstances, while Hawthorn drove lone entries at Aintree and the Tourist Trophy.

For the main discussion, then, I will deal first with the production D-Type as available to the public, and afterwards take up both the factory Le Mans changes and the Cunningham car which Sherwood Johnston drove so well in 1955.

In spite of substantial changes, the chassis-body structure is still by far the most unusual feature of the D Jaguar.

Production cockpit has more elbow room, thanks to frame changes. Horn button is at right of wood-rimmed wheel, "glove box."

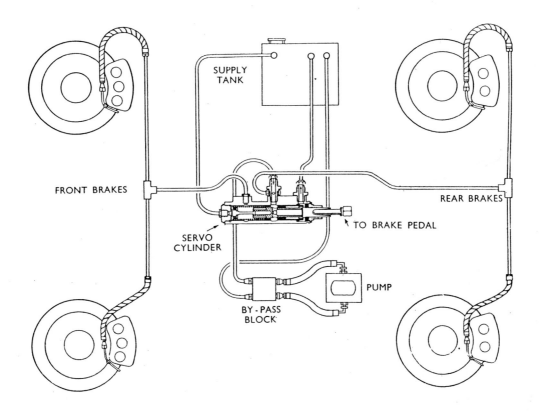

FRONT BRAKES

SUPPLY TANK

REAR BRAKES

SERVO CYLINDER

TO BRAKE PEDAL

BY-PASS BLOCK

PUMP

The central oval cockpit section has holes in the top for the driver and the passenger hatch, and has full bulkheads at front and rear. These are pierced only by the driveshaft in the rear, and the gearbox and driver's feet in the front. Inverted L-shaped boxes are riveted low on each side of the interior, adding greatly to the stiffness of this very light fully-stressed cockpit.

The prototype alloy tubing has given way to 18 and 20 gauge square-section steel tubing, brazed together. This new subframe weighed slightly less than the original, thanks largely to considerable simplification in the cockpit region. Flanged on the bottom to support the floor, the two main tubes sprout from the driveshaft hole in the rear bulkhead and diverge to the lower front suspension mounts. Starting from the same rear point, the upper tubes rise sharply in small section to the front bulkhead, where they enlarge, level out, and diverge similarly to the upper front wishbone mounts. Vertical and lateral bracing at this point unites and stiffens the front end, while two additional large tubes begin at the maximum width of the front bulkhead and converge to a point just behind the radiators. A detachable frame of circular-section tubes carries the oil and water radiators and the hood pivots, while the tubular frame as a whole is merely bolted to the stressed cockpit at the front and rear bulkheads and along the floor, greatly easing repairs.

Four main bolts and an additional series across the top suspend the riveted alloy tail from the rear bulkhead. The tail must support only its own weight and that of the spare

Brakes on Cunningham D-Type have wheel scoops in addition to nose ducting. Wishbones are forged.

The hottest Jaguar

wheel, fuel and tank, and this it does by stressed internal diaphragms instead of a framework as on the prototype. Two horizontal struts below the axle add support in compression. The fuel tank itself is flexible, of "rubberized" fabric, and is housed in an alloy box in the tail.

With the tail removed the D-Type looks odd indeed, since the live axle is suspended directly from the rear bulkhead. Two flat steel trailing arms 16 inches long form a parallelogram on each side, absorbing braking and accelerating torque reactions as well as providing fore-and-aft axle location. The upper arms are simply rubber bushed, while the forward pivots of the bottom arms engage the extremities of a transverse torsion bar through internally-and-externally splined vernier couplings. An enlarged center section of the bar is splined to its surrounding tube, giving, in effect, a separate torsion bar for each wheel. Lateral axle location is looked after by a large A member, with its spex fixing the rear roll center at the differential casing.

The forward ends of the four trailing arms and the pivots of the A member are located on two vertical fabricated posts which are connected at the bottom by the torsion bar housing and the top by a smaller tube. Cirling shocks with built-in bump stops also act from these posts, which in turn are bolted to boxed stiffeners in the rear bulkhead. In action, geometry requires the trailing arms to twist slightly, and their flat section allows this and provides additional roll stiffness.

Praise is due the very neat front suspension, which is one of the cleanest parts of the D Jaguar. Of the well-known parallel wishbone type, it also uses the ball joints that are now common on both sides of the Atlantic. The wishbones themselves are beautifully forged, and the slightly shorter top arm has eccentric and threaded pivots at the frame to allow adjustment of caster and camber. Simple pivots are used for the lower arm, and from them the forward leg of the wishbone extends inward far enough to provide a splined mounting for the forward end of the longitudinal torsion bar, which is not, then, concentric with the bottom arm pivots, and is thus subject to very slight bending. Twenty-four

splines at the forward end and 25 at the frame connection allow a vernier adjustment of height.

An anti-roll bar is now fitted at the front, and Girling shock absorbers again do the job, acting on the lower wishbones. Steering is by rack and pinion, the box sitting high and controlling the wheels by links and arms forward of the wheel center. The steering column is in two sections, with two universal joints in the control shaft.

Also in the chassis department and also unusual are the Dunlop wheels and brakes. That "Indianapolis" look is caused by the pierced aluminum-alloy wheels, which carry a steel center section and five bolts, the domed heads of which engage with holes in a hub

plate and thus transmit braking and drive torque. These increasingly-popular discs are lighter than the equivalent wire type, and are retained by three-lobe locking nuts.

Design of Dunlop disc brakes for competition has reached an initial stage of stability, but many aspects of service are still left to the discretion of the owner. The basic layout first distributes braking effort by providing three pairs of pads for each front disc, and two pairs per wheel at the rear. In the Dunlop system, each pad has its own small hydraulic cylinder, and these are bored in appropriate groups in light alloy blocks, which are separated from the pad-bearing calipers by pylons. Air can thus pass between the pad and the piston, and can keep the hydraulic fluid at a reasonable temperature. Clearance is automatically held around 0.010 of an inch, and 13/16 of an inch of wear are allowed before new pads must be cemented to their carriers. When they have "dished"

much more than 0.020, the discs themselves should be replaced.

Additional proportioning of braking force is effected by the clever and simple servo system. The front section of the servo cylinder is basically an ordinary master cylinder, applying the front brakes only. Behind the piston of this cylinder, fluid is kept continually circulating by a Plessey pump driven from the rear of the gearbox. A take-off from the inlet of this circulating system leads directly to the rear brakes. When the pedal is pressed, the forward piston immediately actuates the front brakes manually, and a rear piston begins to restrict the outlet of the circulating fluid. Pressure is thus built up, which supplements the effort on the front piston and applies the back brakes directly. The degree of restriction can be varied to modify the servo effect.

Front and rear systems are thus hydraulically separate, and the front pads will always be applied if the pressure pump is inoperative. A bypass valve prevents air from being drawn into the system when the car is backing up, and additional mechanical calipers at the rear provide hand braking. The whole servo system is, of course, necessary to avoid excessive pedal travel as a result of feeding twenty wheel cylinders, as well as to make up for the lack of servo in a disc system.

"XK" has been the password at Coventry for seven years, and it still applies to the production D-type engine. The cast iron block, the forged steel connecting rods, and the forged EN-16 steel crankshaft differ only in minor machining from Mark VII parts, while the head is a modified aluminum alloy C-type casting. Vandervell indium-lead-bronze bearings carry the seven main and six rod journals, which are 2.750 and 2.086 of an inch in diameter respectively. The crank is not fully counterweighted, the feeling being that torsional vibration would be more of a problem than bearing loads, and to the same end a large steel vibration damper is fitted at the front. This plus the mass of the special clutch eliminates the need for a separate flywheel.

The two-bolt H-section connecting rod is drilled to lubricate the fully-floating wrist pin, which is held in the full-skirted Aerolite piston by circlips.

A special Dykes design for the centrifugally-cast top rings greatly reduces blow-by at high piston speeds, and a single Maxilite oil control ring is used. Recommended skirt clearance is .006 of an inch, which could probably be almost doubled for shorter races, or for use with hot fuel.

A two-stage Renold duplex roller chain, controlled by a Weller spring tensioner, drives the twin overhead camshafts, which in turn operate the valves through cups sliding in inserted cast iron guides. The cam contours retain the 3/8 lift of the M and C cams, but increase intake duration by 30°, to a total of 270°. Still larger than in older versions, the valves are symmetrically placed with an included angle of 70°, and returned to their seats by double springs. These changes, aided by a 1/2-point compression ratio increase to 9 to 1, have brought the power up 30 bhp from the 220 bhp C-Type.

Basic porting has not changed from the original Weslake layout, the intake passage being slightly curved to provide turbulence. The spark plug is at one side of the hemispherical chamber, in such a position as to produce a flame front moving away from the intake valve. So much room is taken up by the three twin-choke Weber carburetors and their associated plumbing that the engine is canted 8½ degrees to the left on its three-point mounting to allow space at the top. Giving a 45 mm bore and 38 mm choke for each cylinder, the type 45 DC03 Webers supply very accurate mixtures at high lateral G's, thanks to the centrally-disposed emulsion

tubes and jets. Short velocity stacks draw air from a grille-supplied balance box, and fuel arrives via a single flexible line from the two S.U. pumps on the rear bulkhead.

Two three-branch welded exhaust manifolds feed first short flex pipes and then the outside sections, which end just before the rear wheel. Ignition is thoroughly conventional, being by a Lucas single-breaker automatic advance distributor, with a chassis-mounted Lucas HV12 coil.

Partly to facilitate oil cooling, but mainly to reduce engine height by 2¾", a dry-sump oil system is used. A transverse shaft at the front of the engine is gear-driven from the crankshaft, and powers the scavenge pump on the left and the pressure pump on the right. The steel drive gear of the scavenge pump engages with two cast iron idlers, to facilitate the use of two separate oil pickups at front and rear of the shallow sump. This pump attempts to fill the three gallon oil tank, which rests on the left and is vented to the crankcase. The single-idler pressure pump, however, draws from the tank and sends SAE 30 oil at 45/50 psi through the oil cooler and back to a transfer block which then supplies the main gallery. Owners are cautioned to change oil before every race!

Front-end space is shared by the vertical oil radiator and the Marston light-alloy water matrix, which is connected to the separate header tank by two hoses. The tank in turn gets hot water from a gallery cast into the intake "manifold." A pressure valve on the header tank keeps the system under a pressure of around 4 psi, and the operating temperature should be about 70°C.

As mentioned before the D Jag has no flywheel as such, and the pinion of the gearbox-mounted starter engages a ring gear on the clutch body itself. The two metallic driving discs are splined to the outside body, and of the three friction-faced driven discs, two are internally splined to the hub of the third disc, which is splined to the gearbox clutch shaft. A Girling hydraulic unit overcomes the force of six springs and small centrifugal weights to disengage the discs. This type of clutch, while tending to be rough, has favorably small unit and centrifugal loadings.

A wholly new transmission has synchromesh on all four of the helical, constant-mesh gears, and the lowly spur gear survives only in reverse. SAE 30 also is used here, and is a mainshaft eccentric. The short Hardy Spicer drive shaft has a sliding spline and two Hooke-type universal joints.

Another "like-standard" part is the Salisbury differential housing, which carries the hypoid final drive gears. Jaguar recommends that a separate housing be used for each ratio contemplated for competition, to save wear on the tapped holes, and also point out that dimensionally different housings are necessary for ratios above 3.54 and below 3.92. SAE 90 hypoid oil keeps things turning smoothly.

The D-type driver is faced by a 180 mph speedometer and a tach red-lined at 5800 and driven from the left-hand

camshaft. He also knows oil pressure and water temperature but not oil temperature. The interior on the whole is very well finished, and all fuses and junction boxes are readily reached on the passenger's side. No full belly pan is fitted, the engine and drive line being exposed underneath for accessibility and cooling. Oddly enough, the engine must be lowered out of the chassis, and does not just lift the top.

The production D-Type as outlined above is right on a par with the 1954 prototypes and is thus a hot machine in its own right, but Bill Haynes at Jaguar realized that something hotter under the hood would be needed to deal with the SLR Mercedes, so some significant modifications were fitted to the factory cars only in 1955.

Most important was an entirely new head casting, which breathed so well that more power was realized at lower revs, and the peak torque speed raised by 1000 rpm. In the new head, also developed by Harry Weslake, the inlet valve remains inclined at 35° to the vertical, but the exhaust stem now leans out at 40°. Identifiable by a square instead of a circular front inspection plate, the new design did not give complete satisfaction at Le Mans, so the factory decided not to release it quite yet. As a result, little is known about it, but it obviously has longer velocity stacks and almost certainly has much wilder cams and larger, straighter ports. A further refinement is the use of long double exhaust pipes intended to derive an extractor effect from a low pressure area at the rear.

Body changes were also in order, to improve already fine streamlining and give better driver protection. To these ends the nose was lengthened 7½ inches and fitted with brake cooling ducts, while the windshield was raised and faired back into a higher and cleaner fin. After some prolonged pit stops in 1954, an exceptionally large fuel filter was fitted in the cockpits of the 1955 team cars.

Briggs Cunningham's Le 'Mans Jaguar was privately owned, and as such could not use the prototype head that was allowed the factory machines. His car therefore was a production car in all respects save the nose and tail, which gave it the "team car" look. Once in this country, the D proved very difficult to handle on characteristically tight American courses. Excessive understeer (for Le Mans stability) made it tough to haul around corners, so the Cunningham team went to work.

They fitted soft, sticky Pirelli tires in the front, and harder Firestones in the rear, also cutting the front tire section to 5.50. More interesting, they con-

Jaguar

nected the two bottom rear trailing arms with a torsion anti-rolling bar, sensibly decreasing the rear cornering power. Both at Nassau and Palm Springs D-Types have suffered from lateral stabilizer failure, a weak point shown up by much more strenuous U. S. cornering conditions.

Short courses are also hard on brakes, and a disc can't dissipate heat without an air supply, so the front ducts are supplemented by 1954-type scoops. New ducting clamped to the axle tubes also picks up air from beneath the car and directs it on the leading edge of the rear discs. Just in case, a radiator blind is fitted that pulls down from the top window-shade-fashion and can be controlled from the cockpit.

Johnston didn't go over 6300 rmp at Nassau, and yet managed to break up the front connecting rod. On the other hand, Moss ran his engine up to 7200 in the '54 Le Mans, probably on the overrun when suffering from bad brakes, and didn't bust anything. The factory recommends that speeds above 5750 rpm be held for short periods only, and that upshifts be made at 5500. Gearing should allow the D to reach but not exceed 5800 on the straights. 5750 rpm move the pistons at 4000 feet per minute, which is a reasonable limit for the present-day engine, and exceptional for a ten-year old concept.

Attempts at prediction are always risky, but if Jaguar enters the 1956 Le Mans under the announced proto-type rules, they might do well by adding long-awaited fuel injection to the 2.5 litre block that was tried in the 1954 Tourist Trophy and later ap-

peared in the "2.4" sedan. Such a combo would be good for 100 bhp per litre anyway, and should wind up like a buzz saw. The great value of the Jaguar standard line is in no small way related to the lessons learned from such fabulously fast road machines as the hottest Jag: the D-Type.

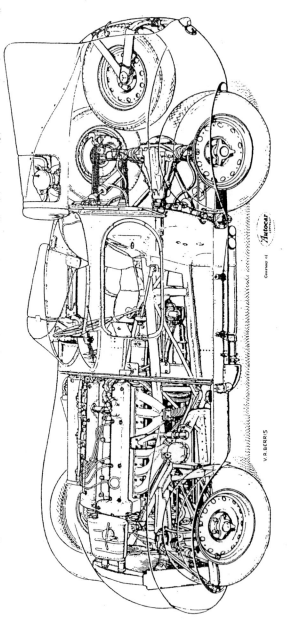

Courtesy of *Autocar*

V.R. BERRIS

THE D TYPE JAGUAR

CONNELL

ROAD TESTING THE *D-JAGUAR*

"A THRILL THAT comes once in a life-time" is an overworked cliché, but it describes pefectly our impressions after conducting a full-scale road test on the D-type Jaguar.

This is the best performing automobile we have ever tested, and we've tested some very potent machinery. An acceleration time from a standstill to 60 mph in under 5 seconds, or to 100 mph in just over 12 seconds is startling enough, but this is combined with a genuine timed top speed of 162 mph!

We did not drive the test car, nor did we run any fuel consumption checks. The car itself was provided by Pearce Woods, of Continental Motors in Whittier, Calif. On very short notice, Mr. Woods agreed with us that the true potential of this car should be made public. He and two mechanics arose at 5:00 A.M., and 4 hours later we had all the data we needed.

Some of the technical problems encountered when recording the true performance of a car of this calibre are rather difficult. For example, no two starts are ever quite alike, and too much throttle is very hard on the clutch, or gives too much initial wheelspin. Insufficient throttle and too rapid clutch engagement gives a momentary stumble after the first few feet of travel. Once underway the speedometer needle sweeps around the dial so rapidly that it is almost impossible to record the times for zero to 30 and zero ot 40 mph. The times to 60 mph varied from 4.2 seconds to 5.0 seconds, but the average of four trials was 4.7 seconds. Accordingly, no data is given in the panel for 0-to-30 or 0-to-40 mph, but the plot of acceleration indicates times of about 2.0 and 3.1 seconds, respectively. Three runs over the standing ¼ mile averaged 13.7 seconds, with the best run at 13.5 seconds. This time is plotted on our usual acceleration graph (see arrow) and shows that the true speed at the end of the quarter was very close to 107 mph.

The timed top speed of this particular car is given as 162 mph. How this run was made will be described, but the exact spot is our secret. The time was 8:30 on a Sunday morning. The altitude was sea level, temperature 60°F, wind zero, visibility less than a mile (fog, not smog). Two high speed runs were made, the first with the Editor alongside Pearce Woods. Because the passenger has no wind deflector of any kind, goggles are a necessity, and the seat cushions were removed so that only his head appeared. To avoid all possibility of missing the markers at each end of the ¼ mile strip, a man was stationed at each end. We used a run of just under 2 miles to get up speed and the tach read 6500 rpm at the 1½ mile mark. It would go no further and the run was timed by three syncronized watches at 155.17 mph. For the second run (the Editor had had enough) the cockpit cover was installed and the spark advance was retarded slightly. It was a thrilling sight to watch, though at first there was no car in view—just the distant scream of an engine winding up in each gear. Then suddenly a tiny white car appeared out of the mist, and as it shrieked towards us it seemed literally to be a blur as it sped straight and true down the highway. The tell-tale hand on the tachometer was at 6600 rpm and the true recorded speed was exactly 162.16 mph! Whether the extra 7 mph was due to less wind resistance or to the change in spark advance is anyone's guess, though the lower drag theory seems logical.

Mr. Woods and his crew do not subscribe to the theory that only the factory (necessarily) knows what is best for this car as to gear ratios, safe maximum rpm, or even assembling and tuning the engine. This applies particularly to racing on this continent, under our special conditions and with our fuels. The factory is very specific about safe max. revolutions: 5800 rpm and no more. However the factory team cars use much more than this, even at Le Mans, and if one can afford the risk of occasional "expensive noises," the chances are that much better for success. This engine was set up with somewhat looser clearances throughout than recommended, and incorporated minor changes in the lubrication system including higher oil pressure. The non-standard axle gears are American Spicer and require extensive machine work to adapt. Much of the success of this car is attributed to its axle ratio (3.54 is standard on all D-Jags, 2.92 and 3.31 are factory options), to the larger than standard Pirelli rear tires and to the engine's ability to withstand up to 6600 rpm occasionally (a piston speed of 4580 fpm!) The 7.00″ section tires used in place of the standard 6.50″ size reduce engine revs per mile by about 5.5%. In other words the engine revs per mile are almost exactly the same as given by the standard set-up. We can safely claim, therefore, that the performance data obtained is truly representative and typical of a standard D-type Jaguar. However, it must be remembered that the factory cars have special cylinder heads and other undisclosed changes which add 35 bhp and give 9.5% more torque. It is interesting to compare this car's performance to that of our best previous test, the 2.9 Ferrari reported in our May, 1954 issue.

	D-Jag	2.9 Ferrari
0-60	4.7 secs.	5.1 secs.
0-80	8.0	8.5
0-100 mph	12.1	13.7
SS ¼	13.7	14.4
Tapley (4th)	480 lbs/ton	380 lbs/ton
bhp	250	240
torque	242 ft-lbs	178 ft-lbs
axle ratio	3.73	4.25
top speed	162 mph	135 mph
Drag at 60	80 lbs	123 lbs.
Test weight	2460 lbs	2350 lbs.

(Continued on page 54)

ROAD & TRACK ROAD TEST NO. F-6-56

JAGUAR D—TYPE

SPECIFICATIONS

List price	$9875
Wheelbase	90.6 in.
Tread, front	50 in.
rear	50 in.
Tire size (rear)	7.00-16
Curb weight	not checked
Test weight (est.)	2460 lbs.
Engine	6-cyl.
Valves	dohc
Bore & stroke	3.27 x 4.17 in.
Displacement	3442 cc
Compression ratio	9.00
Horsepower	250
peaking speed	6000
equivalent mph	139
Torque, ft-lbs	242
peaking speed	4000
equivalent mph	92.5
Mph per 1000 rpm	23.2
Mph at 2500 fpm	83.5
Gear ratios (overall)	
4th	3.73
3rd	4.78
2nd	6.14
1st	7.99
R&T high gear performance factor	85.0

PERFORMANCE

Timed top speed	162
Max. speeds in gears—	
3rd (6200)	112
2nd (6200)	87
1st (6200)	67
Shift points from—	
same as above.	
Mileage range	not checked

ACCELERATION

0-50 mph	3.9 secs.
0-60 mph	4.7 secs.
0-70 mph	6.4 secs.
0-80 mph	8.0 secs.
0-90 mph	10.1 secs.
0-100 mph	12.1 secs.
Standing ¼ mile	13.7 secs.
best run	13.5 secs.

TAPLEY READINGS

Gear	Lbs/ton	Mph	Mph/sec.
1st	off-scale	—	—
2nd	off-scale	—	—
3rd	600	72	6.1
4th	480	93	4.8
Total drag at 60 mph, 80 lbs.			

SPEEDO ERROR

Indicated	Actual
30 mph	27.6
40 mph	35.8
50 mph	43.2
60 mph	51.6
70 mph	60.0
80 mph	68.2
90 mph	77.0
100 mph	87.5
110 mph	97.8

D-TYPE JAGUAR
acceleration through the gears
(with special 3.73 axle)